DATE DUE

MAY 6 1995			
NOV 9 1996			

On Writing the
COLLEGE APPLICATION
ESSAY

ON WRITING THE
COLLEGE
APPLICATION
ESSAY

by Harry Bauld

BARNES & NOBLE BOOKS
A DIVISION OF HARPER & ROW, PUBLISHERS

NEW YORK, CAMBRIDGE, PHILADELPHIA, SAN FRANCISCO
WASHINGTON, LONDON, MEXICO CITY, SÃO PAULO
SINGAPORE, SYDNEY

FIRST EDITION

Designer: Ruth Bornschlegel

Copy Editor: Mary Jane Alexander

Library of Congress Cataloging-in-Publication Data

Bauld, Harry.
  On writing the college application essay.

  1. College applictions. 2. Exposition (Rhetoric). 3. Universities and colleges—Admission. I. Title.
LB2351.5.B38   1987   378'.1057   86–46043
ISBN 0–06–055076–7   87 88 89 90 91 MPC 10 9 8 7 6 5 4 3 2 1
ISBN 0–06–463722–0 (pbk.)   87 88 89 90 91 MPC 10 9 8 7 6 5 4 3 2 1

95588

*To Ursula Cino
and Martha Straus*

And because I found I had nothing else to
write about, I presented myself as a subject.

Montaigne

Contents

READING

Acknowledgments

This book would not have been possible without the direct and indirect help of many friends and former colleagues in admissions and in teaching. I would like to thank the two admissions directors who hired me and from whom I learned much about the mysteries of selection, Bill Oliver of Columbia and Jim Rogers of Brown. My friends Jim McMenamin and Larry Momo of Columbia also instructed me in the admissions sciences, and read portions of the manuscript. Thanks also to Beth Janes of the Middlesex School for her good sense and plain talk.

My gratitude is great to the faculty and staff of the Horace Mann School in New York, especially to Mike Lacopo, now headmaster of the Isidore Newman School, who convinced me that teaching might be worthwhile, and to Kristin Crowley in college placement, who contributed her time and insight to the book. It is impossible to name everyone who made teaching at Horace Mann the pleasure it was, but to all my friends there I offer the fondest thanks.

I'm indebted to Sally Goldfarb for expertise legal and literary, and to Nathan and Betty Straus for their suggestions on the manuscript. I'm also grateful to Gary Cornog of the Millbrook School for testing parts of it in his classroom.

John and Julie Kronenberger, Chris Daly, Anne Fishel, Irv Schenkler, Nancy Henry, David and Nina Schiller, Jerry Kisslinger, Eleanor Cornog, Jane and Ben Momo, Steve Bauld, and the members of the Penultimate Society helped more than they know.

Thanks also to Marian Young, writer's advocate, and to Jeanne Flagg at Harper & Row, who saw the potential early on.

Most of all I wish to express appreciation to the Horace Mann students I taught and who taught me, and to acknowledge those whose writing appears in this book: Rani Arbo, Amherst '89; Melanie Berger, Harvard '90; Roland Davis, Harvard '90; Gerard Greweldinger, Amherst '89; Carolyn Grose, Middlebury '88; Jennifer Gross, Brown '89; Sharon Isaak, Princeton '91; Justine Klineman, Dartmouth '89; Nicole Parisier, Harvard '89; Ghita Schwarz, Harvard '90; Rebecca Shannon, Harvard '89; Meredith Wollins, Carnegie Mellon '89. Their work appears with their permission.

John Bailo, Princeton '82, has also kindly granted permission to use his college essay.

Introduction

On a fall day not long ago I returned to the high school where I once taught English, to "address the senior class." (In the past I simply talked to students, but it seems any time you travel more than 150 miles to say something you are entitled to a lot more respect.)

The place was packed; even students who had cut my classes were there, looking angelic and attentive. There was a reason for that, I knew. My subject was College Admissions.

I hadn't even finished panting from the four-flight trudge up to the auditorium before a girl stood up in the middle of the crowd and asked The Question.

"What are they looking for on those application essays, anyway?"

I've faced that same query hundreds of times in the last eight years, and I've always been tempted to mimic the Zen master who, when asked "What is Zen?" by his students, simply put his slippers on his head and left the room. But Western sympathy has prevailed and I've stayed behind with my shoes on, trying to explain why "What are they looking for?"—like "What's going to be on the test?"—is an Unquestion, or at least the wrong question.

This book will help you ask (and answer) the right questions. There are two reasons for you to concentrate on your essay. Number One you may already be intimately acquainted with: it's not easy. (The Princeton application admits in its instructions for the essay that "This may be the most difficult part of the application." That really gets those creative juices flowing, doesn't it?) In fact, it's a pain in at least two anatomical areas. As an admissions officer, I've seen the doom and dismay in the faces of thousands of applicants who've asked me about the essay, and as a teacher I've watched my students agonize over them. (Once, not so many years ago, I even wrote a couple of college essays myself.) So I know it's the hardest part of applying, even more grinding than the SAT, which at least *ends* after three hours. Finishing an essay seems to take forever, and there are always more interesting things to do, like daydreaming or eating ice cream sandwiches.

But the second reason to concentrate on it is a happy one. The essay can be your ticket out of the faceless applicant hordes and into First Choice University. And unlike everything else in your application—the grades, recommendations, and tests, which are by now out of your hands—you have real control over your writing, right up to the last frantic minute. Essays show the admissions committee who you are, and it's your chance to let fly, uninterrupted.

You may be more frightened than excited by that opportunity. Many of my students, facing the task at first, have shrugged and said, "Well, I'm not much of a writer anyway. I speak better than I write. I'll concentrate on the interview." But, as you'll see in chapter one, pinning your hopes on the interview is not a good idea.

My students' doubts about themselves were reflected in the advice of some adults I talked to when I began this book, who suggested I'd have to write "down" toward some Common Denominator. The way they described it, this Common Denominator must have one set of knuckles wrapped around a blunt Crayola and the other dragging on the ground.

But I don't believe I have to write down. Even though we're all swamped every day with sloppy and deceitful language and bad writing, you can learn to say something simple and meaningful—and that's all a college essay asks. Just as my students did, you can write a good one that distinguishes you from everybody else. What nobody can do is just "dash it off." In fact, before you even put pen to application there are two things you must do to help yourself:

*1. Read other essays.*Familiarity breeds knowledge. Every writer working in a special form—sonnet, mystery novel, diet book, college essay—needs to know how it has been handled in the past, the good and the bad. Being able to navigate around the dangerous shoals of cliché and convention is a necessity for the sailor in college-essay waters. Chapters three, nine, eleven, and twelve, as well as the sample essays throughout, are maps of previous voyages along this course. Chapter eleven especially, with comments from admissions officers on student essays, will show you routes of clear sailing as well as the dangerous reefs.

*2. Practice.*On your maiden voyage, don't expect to win the America's Cup. You need some practice—the more the better. I have made a few suggestions for ways to strengthen your writing muscles, and even given specific examples. To write well, you have to write. How good you want your college essay to be is up to you.

Throughout the book I concentrate on the writing of a general personal statement, to satisfy questions like "Tell us anything you think we should know." But chapter ten lists both common and unusual essay questions, as well as a few methods for recycling your personal statement to fit the more gaudy requests. Even though many schools change their essay assignments from year to year, you can analyze them using the methods in chapter ten.

A warning: There's no magic formula for writing the college essay. "Writing," said E. B. White, "is an act of faith, not a trick of grammar." It's not any kind of trick at all, in fact. Your writing is your way of seeing and of thinking, and good college essays have as many guises as the Greek god Proteus, who was always changing shape to slip out of somebody's grasp. You, as a college essayist, must realize how *protean* you can be, too: one minute telling a story, the next confessing and explaining a bias, or reminiscing, or investigating your world like a reporter. All so that you can slip *into* somebody's grasp.

A word about the examples. Whether a particular essay "worked," no one can say, if by worked we mean it was the crowbar that opened the gate. Some essays, no matter how good, won't get you into First Choice University; some, no matter how bad, won't keep you out (if your parents just gave a million dollars to remodel the admissions building, let's say). The essays in this book are naturally taken out of their application contexts, so you don't know who had three A's senior year and who was captain of cross-country. It's not always easy to tell precisely why someone "got in." But a good essay, like a good painting, has an interior rightness that has nothing to do with the price it fetches in the college admissions auction. That rightness makes the difference for you when the decision could go either way. If you write as well as you can, the rest of the process will take care of itself, and you can glide into your senior spring knowing you'll be more than just a pile of papers to the admissions committee.

That's how an essay really *works:* it shows you at your alive and thinking best, a person worth listening to—not just for the ten minutes it takes to read your application, but for the next four years.

GETTING READY

1 The Gray Area

OK, so you're not a straight-A student in Phillips Andover's toughest program, captain of three sports, with 1500 SATs and a great-grandfather who was the seventh president of Harvard College; you're not the caboose in your class either. If you're like most of the hundreds of thousands of applicants to selective colleges every year, you fall into that murky netherworld peopled by those whose credentials are neither easily accepted nor easily denied: the Gray Area.

But don't panic. Everyone's in the Gray Area *somewhere.* (Well, almost everyone. If the hot-shot profile above could be you, put this book back on the shelf. As long as you don't write an essay about the pleasures of sticking pins into small furry animals, you're Harvard bound.) In fact, things get a bit grayer if you're not from one of the built-in Lobby Groups in the process: recruited athletes, development prospects (people who can spare a few million in pocket change to build a new gymnasium), members of a federally designated minority group, or children of alumni. All these applicants have special advocates for them in close contact with the admissions committee. Everybody else is Just Folks.

Just Folks are often suspicious that quotas exist for the Lobbies (and so for Just Folks), but quotas are almost completely gone from the admissions scene. At the most competitive schools, the percentages of Lobby admissions vary from year to year depending on the number of applicants and the needs of the college. But no college pretends its process is "fair." An example of the way it really works is this: Three goalies have been convinced by the hockey coach to apply. The coach's current goalie is a senior, and the backup is a junior. Result: at least one of the goalies applying is going to get in. Period. His grades and test scores may be much worse than hundreds of Just Folks who've already been rejected, but it doesn't matter—the hockey team needs a goalie.

Of course, plenty of applicants from the Lobbies are in the Gray Area too—those other two goalies, for instance. Still, at a college like Amherst, which in 1986 had 4,580 applications for 409 places (they admit about 900, knowing more than half will go elsewhere), after the admissions office finishes with the Lobbies there's hardly anything but scraps left for Just Folks. Practically everyone's in the Gray Area at Amherst—as well as at many other colleges with similar selection ratios.

At best, life in the Gray Area means the admissions committee suspects you're someone who can do the work and even do it well at their school; at worst it means you are indistinguishable from the lump of other students with similar backgrounds and credentials who clog their application pool.

So just getting into the Gray Area at your first-choice school can be something of an accomplishment. The trick, of course, is getting out of the gray shadows of sameness and into the sunlight of acceptance. To do that, you have to become three-dimensional to the committee. The best way: write a good essay. But first you have to understand the essay in context.

Is it the most important part of the application? No. Don't be under any illusions about that. If you *are* choo-chooing along contentedly at the tail end of your class, even the snappiest essay won't deliver you to an Ivy League station.

THE TRANSCRIPT

The honor of "most important part of your application" belongs to your high school transcript. Admissions officers, in sickness and in health, cherish this document above all others. They begin with questions about the courses themselves. Are they solid or soft? You don't need to plow through every honors and advanced placement class offered at your school, but courses like "Feelings" or "Elvis in History" set off the Marshmallow Alert. Admissions officers are also highly suspicious of topics best left to the colleges, like Psychology, Human Ecology, or Aesthetics. In high school, these courses are 99 percent mental bubblegum. If by some miracle they are rigorous at your school, talk to your counselor to make sure the colleges know it. In general, stick with bread-and-butter courses, and advanced levels of them if you're interested.

After checking the difficulty of your program, admissions officers naturally want to know about your grades. (I'm misleading you deliberately here. They don't really look at courses first, grades second; that would be impossible. But showing it this way does give you an idea of an admissions officer's priorities.) In any case, by the time you begin hacking away at your essay, there's nothing left to do about your transcript but smile.

THE SAT: FADING FAST

Admissions officers have always looked on the Scholastic Aptitude Test with a healthy skepticism. They have seen too many students with SATs 100–200 points below the class average—students they were admitting under pressure from Lobbies—wind up four years later in the Cum Laude lists, or go on to become alumni who support the college financially. But recently the SAT is coming under public fire because of the success of Stanley Kaplan's SAT course and those of similar test-prep companies. If these courses *can* help raise scores, critics ask, then how much "aptitude" does the SAT measure?

What the SAT actually measures is debatable. Admissions officers treat it as a test of neither aptitude nor intelligence, nor even as a reliable predictor of success in college. To them, it is simply a reflection of your achievement versus your background. In other words, a 580 verbal from a Chicago private-school girl whose parents, both lawyers, went to Harvard is not the same as a 580 verbal from a Mississippi farm girl whose home contains two books—*TV Guide* and the Bible. One is commonplace, the other extraordinary.

A few colleges, like Bowdoin, have eliminated the SAT from

their decision making, and even schools that use it know that a score means only a range of plus or minus thirty points. For instance, 580 really means 550–610. The SAT is not in the same league as your transcript in predicting your college performance.

But remember—even the transcript and SAT together don't tell your whole story to the admissions committee. At Brown, we routinely turned down students with superb grades and high test scores. "What does he offer us," we would ask, "besides numbers?" The kicker for the college admissions committee is still their personal response to you, the flesh on the statistical bones. Where do they find the real you?

THE MYTH OF THE INTERVIEW

Not (usually) in the interview. Hard to believe, but true. Unlike employers, even the most competitive colleges use interviews more for public relations than evaluations. Interviewers are under strict orders to be charming and warm, no matter what they think of a candidate. The object of an interview, from the college's point of view, is to give you a terrific experience of their school. It's a recruiting tool. (After all, you may get in.) You're not likely to get the legendary medical-school interview questions, like, "What kind of vegetable would you like to be—and why?" No one is going to ask you to open a window that's secretly been nailed shut, just to see your reaction. At least, no good interviewer will ask these things. So relax on your interview—as long as you don't drool, you'll be fine.

Why does the interview count so little? One reason is that many interviews are done by alumni, graduate students, even undergraduates (that's how I got my start in admissions), and admissions officers can't depend on these impressions. They don't even know all their interviewers personally. Another reason is that one terror-filled conversation can hardly outweigh four years of achievement. Interviews simply contain too many variables. More than one Ivy League admissions director has told me he would cut out campus interviews altogether—they take up too much staff time gathering largely useless information—except that parents and students would raise an outcry, unwilling to believe in the unimportance of those thirty white-knuckled minutes.

TEACHER RECOMMENDATIONS

But admissions officers are looking for the real you, not a statistical profile. If not in the interview, where do they find you? One place is in the teacher recommendations, but these are only as good as the teachers writing them. Their influence varies according to how well the writers know you and how clearly they can paint a portrait of you for a reader. Some recommendations are crucial in a decision; others are meaningless.

Incidentally, here's how to pick a teacher to write your recommendations. Don't automatically go for the one who gave you an A. You want someone who knows you well and writes well. In an ideal world, you could evaluate samples of their writing beforehand, but here on earth asking for such a thing might put a wee strain on teacher-student relations. In place of samples you can make an educated guess about their writing based on their teaching styles. Good teachers are usually good because they communicate vividly and so are a good bet to write well. Beware the recommendation from the dull, indifferent teacher, the one you secretly know is mediocre or worse (alas, they exist), even though you aced the course. It will read, "Susan is a fine student and a fine person who is very thorough and completes all her work on time and with neatness. She is well-groomed," etc.

You don't want *that*. What you need is intelligence and authority in your recommendation, a letter that will make you come alive—the same vividness you're searching for in your own essay writing. Once you have such a teacher or teachers in mind, you naturally want to know whether they'll support you strongly or not. But don't ask, "Will you write me a good recommendation?" After such a crass question, which puts the teacher in the ugly position of deciding whether or not to be your shill, the chances that it *will* be a good one decrease quickly. Instead, ask "Would you write my college recommendation?" The following answers bode well:

"Sure."

"I'd be happy to."

"Certainly."

And similar responses, given *without hesitation.* If there is any throat clearing or paper shuffling, find someone else. For instance, the teacher might begin with a slow, "Well . . ." or an "I'll tell you what—"

"No problem," you say, smile, and skip out into the hallway to be alone with your disappointment. It's hard to take these little rejections, but it's a lot easier than taking a big one from First Choice U. because your recommendations were lukewarm. If he or she says, "Have you tried someone else? If you get stuck, come back to me," don't ever come back. That way rejection lies. Read faces. If the expression says, I have so much work that I am in physical pain at the idea of this new burden, excuse yourself quickly and say, "That's OK, I have some other people lined up." If you have trouble finding someone who knows you, you've been doing something wrong at school.

PUBLISH OR PERISH

In the admissions committee's search for who you are, the essay is, in fact, no more important than any other part of the application, with this important difference: it's the only place they can hear *your voice,* just as you want it. One big difficulty with that is obvious: you've probably never written anything like this, and certainly not for an audience you can't (and may never) see. It's not the same as the history paper for Mr. Snoozleman on the causes of the Civil War, or the English assignment for Ms. Hackenbush on the significance of the green light at the end of the dock in *The Great Gatsby.* In those assignments, Mr. Snoozleman and Ms. Hackenbush aren't waiting breathlessly to read your words in order to learn something themselves or take pleasure in what you say; they have probably studied these topics for years. At best such assignments are *exercises,* literary pushups supposedly in preparation for college, but meaningless in themselves. At worst, writing them is not writing at all—you're more like a cat in a lab, coughing up hairballs.

But your college essay is not an exercise; it's the Big Game itself. It is, in fact, a piece of "published" writing. Like a book or magazine article, it goes out into a world of unknown readers who will judge you without being on your side from the beginning, the way a teacher is. In fact, it disappears into the hellish hole of the admissions office, never to resurface.

Admissions officers are not your friends. (See all those boxes and checklists they give your counselor and teacher to check off in the recommendations? The colleges are trying to get your counselor and teacher to do the admissions officer's job, which is to rate the candidates. Those boxes don't help *you*.) Although they are not your friends, they know more about you than some of your friends—and most of your teachers. At most colleges, the materials in your file are placed in a strict order, beginning with your "numbers": class rank and SATs, which often go on the outside of the folder. The first forms inside contain information about your family and your parents' employment and education, followed by the transcript, counselor's report, and teacher recommendations. *Then* comes your part of the application. By the time admissions officers get to your essay, they know your family and your schoolwork very well. They already know a great deal about your school, and they're seeing certain patterns about you.

Understanding all this may seem only to add to your nervous procrastination at first. But you'll be able to use this knowledge to advantage if you approach your college essay the way published writers approach their work:

1. Who is my audience?
2. What kind of piece is it?
3. What do I have to say to these readers? (*Not*, What do they want to hear?)

Begin at the beginning. Who are these people who hold your fate in their hands? Now that you know where your essay fits into the application, let's find out where it fits into an admissions officer's life.

Steel yourself and proceed.

2 Know Your Audience

At eight P.M. in the bleak heart of winter the bundled figure of a wretched man, perhaps the village bum, drags itself like a troll across the frozen campus of First Choice University in the town of Crewneck, Massachusetts. His hunch and eyes of despair speak of sleepless nights, probably on doorstoops and benches. In his right hand is an enormous stained and beat-up canvas bag, its handle frayed and unraveling, the weight of its contents making him list to starboard like a sloop in a squall; it might contain all his worldly possessions—at least the ones he isn't wearing. He makes a pitiful picture.

Yet a closer look under the lowered hat brim reveals an alarmingly young face for one on the fritz. The eyes are full of fatigue, yes, but a peek into his bag reveals no cardboard shoes, half-empty nips, salvaged mosquito netting, nor any of the other sad accessories of street living. Inside the bag, instead, are stacks and stacks of manila folders covered in cryptic scrawls—applications for admission to First Choice University. This prematurely aged man is twenty-five years old, and he is neither drunk nor destitute. At this late hour on this bitter night, he is just leaving work. His name is Henry Haggard, and he is an admissions officer in the middle of application-reading season.

Poor Henry is not looking forward to the rest of the evening. While many of his non-admissions friends in Crewneck are already out to dinner and frolic this Thursday night—the beginning of the weekend in all college towns—he still has thirty applications to read by tomorrow. His lone hope for combining business with pleasure is to find others who can share in and sympathize with his drudgery. That leaves only the other members of the admissions staff, with whom he already spends twenty-four hours a day, it seems. But then he thinks of the newest admissions officer, a young woman just graduated from First Choice last spring . . . Let's fast-forward to later that evening.

SCENE: The living room of Haggard's apartment, decorated with a week's worth of crumpled socks lying across the unmatched secondhand furniture like dead herring. Smashed Doritos mingled with rug lint form a crunchy veneer underfoot. In one corner, a tiny television crackles with a basketball game. Henry is stretched out half-awake on the couch, shifting restlessly. Now and then he lifts a manila folder from the pile that reaches up beside him a foot high, looks wearily through its contents, writes something in pencil inside, and heaves it to the floor. He has spent most of his evenings this month—in fact the last four winters of his life—in this position. In his imagination tonight the inside of his refrigerator looms in Technicolor, the frosted green glass of the beer bottles beckoning to him like beautiful mermaids across an endless murky gulf of application forms.

On the other side of the room, sunk in a low-slung armchair, is Sarah Bleary—twenty-one, bright, attractive, but already sprouting dark circles under the eyes in this, her first admissions season. Pencil in hand, she stares stonily at the contents of a folder from a pile of her own, as high as Haggard's. The two of them push at the papers like drugged seals. Their eyes are glassy from long hours of close work.

BLEARY: You sure know how to show a girl a good time.

HAGGARD: Welcome to life in the admissions office.

BLEARY: Hey, here's an essay for you. *(He does not look up. She reads from the application.)* "I believe diversity of learning is the most important educational goal to have—"

HAGGARD *(putting his hands over his ears):* No more, I can't take it. Not while the Celtics are down ten points.

BLEARY *(going on):* "For me, diversity has a double advantage: Firstly, it is to anyone's advantage to know about as much as they can, and secondly, there are more than one or two things in which I am interested. I am not saying that it is not good to concentrate studies in one area later on, or that I want to learn all there is to learn, but rather that my four college years will be my chance to take a wider range of courses than I ever could, and I intend to take this opportunity." No E. B. White, is he?

HAGGARD: The imagination of a hockey puck.

BLEARY: I've been reading ones like these all night. But the thing is, he's a decent kid—I want to like him.

HAGGARD: There's your first mistake.

BLEARY *(intent on the application):* He's got OK grades in a good courseload at a good school, active enough, but just so gray on paper. He wouldn't stand out against a cement wall.

HAGGARD: Here's your write-up. *(eyes closed, dictating)* "Respectable stats and the usual range of x-currics but bland bland bland. Teachers mention imagination and sense of humor not confirmed by essay. A numbers call at the end, but looks like WL at best."

BLEARY: How can you say that without even reading the file? Besides, you're wrong about the imagination and humor. They say he's earnest and hard-working.

HAGGARD: So change it to, "Implied drudgery is indeed confirmed by essay." I know that kid and thousands like him. Standard fare from private schools in Boston or New York or Chicago—

BLEARY: It's Dallas, actually.

HAGGARD: Same difference. Probably has New York parents.

BLEARY *(confirming it in the file):* All right, smart guy—

HAGGARD: Or maybe he's from high-tax-bracket public schools in the middle-class 'burbs. Big difference, right? What's so likable?

BLEARY: A little cynical, aren't we?

HAGGARD: Just realistic. Wait'll you've been at it a couple of years. Or months. *The kids gotta come across on paper,* or else when they come up for committee decision you—and they—won't have a leg to stand on. I mean, I like to discover an NSTK as much as anyone—

BLEARY: NSTK?

HAGGARD: Neat Small Town Kid. But even they gotta come alive in the app. Haven't you noticed that most apps are the same as most others? These are teenagers, after all. I know they've really worked hard as assistant business manager of the newspaper and they're all individuals and "very unique"and all of that crap—at least, that's what they all say—but you wouldn't know it from their applications. And that's what counts. I've got no patience for the No-Pulse Brigade.

BLEARY *(yawning):* What time is it?

HAGGARD *(cheering up):* Party time. Want a beer?

BLEARY: No, thanks. *(She pats the top of her pile of folders.)* Duty still beckons.

HAGGARD: Duty doesn't have to be *total* agony.

BLEARY: Yeah, well. I've been on this same kid for half an hour and I can't remember a thing about him. I think I'll get some more coffee.

HAGGARD: Why don't you cut out the middle man and go straight to the No-Doz? There's not enough coffee in Brazil to keep you alert for forty folders. Have a beer—might as well enjoy yourself.

BLEARY: Don't try to corrupt me—I'm on a strict caffeine and popcorn diet. Besides, I'll fall asleep.

HAGGARD: That never stopped anyone from reading folders. Sure, you'll have the occasional nightmare that every kid is a pre-some-thing-or-other whose essay begins, "Hello, I am a very unique person," but you'll get over it. Some of my best evaluations were written asleep. It's like the Ouija board. The pencil moves by itself. *(He struggles up from the couch and goes into the kitchen.)*

BLEARY: How do people do this job for ten or fifteen years?

HAGGARD *(from the kitchen)*: Don't ask me.

BLEARY: Didn't I hear this was your last year?

HAGGARD: Yup. My hitch for Mother First Choice is over. *(returning with coffeepot and two beer bottles)* Law school, here I come.

BLEARY: It's not over yet.

HAGGARD: True. *(He holds out a bottle.)* Brought one for you just in case. Sure you don't want some? *(She shakes her head. He pours from the coffeepot into her cup.)*

BLEARY: Maybe a sip of yours. *(He hands her the beer; she sips and gives it back).* Mmmm.

HAGGARD *(prone again)*: I'll tell you how they do it. The big wheels don't read as many folders, for one thing.

BLEARY: Assistant directors do.

HAGGARD *(sitting up halfway)*: Hey, *I'm* an assistant director. Assistant director means squat. You'll be assistant director too if you stay around two, three years and don't have any major screw-ups. I mean the directors and associate directors, the honchos. You think they read half the folders you do? No way. Too much burnout.

BLEARY: What I can't believe is the amount of paperwork, all the computer junk. I guess I thought of it as mostly meeting kids and parents, choosing the class, that kind of thing. There're plenty of good parts, like all the expense-account travel—

HAGGARD: Join the admissions office and see Tulsa.

BLEARY *(ignoring him):* —and the long vacation, and the people. It's a great job for someone just out of school. But there's a lot of diddly detail, too. I mean, we're talking petty bureaucracy here.

HAGGARD: You got it. Today was typical. I spent most of the morning returning alumni phone calls and talking to guidance counselors, doing two interviews, dictating a letter to a great kid I saw in Colorado, and reading precisely three folders. In the afternoon I had to finish filling out my travel vouchers and writing the reports on my last trip, had a meeting with the Chicano student caucus on recruiting in the southwest, and then we had that full staff meeting at the end. Total folder reading: six. Thirty-four to go—not counting the ones I had left over from yesterday and the day before that.

BLEARY: You're behind?

HAGGARD: Sure.

BLEARY: I thought I was the only one.

HAGGARD: Everybody is. I wouldn't worry about it too much. Everything is designed to get in the way of folder reading.

BLEARY: Including bull sessions like this?

HAGGARD: Hey, oxen get to take the yoke off once in a while. How far behind are you?

BLEARY: Far.

HAGGARD: How long does it take you to do a folder?

BLEARY: I don't know, fifteen minutes or so, with writing it up and everything. I guess longer when I get tired.

HAGGARD: Well, there it is. Not bad, but you've gotta do five or six an hour to keep from drowning. Ten minutes and get outta there. And hell, even that doesn't do it. What you realize is that, to do the job right, there aren't enough hours. And that is why God invented winter weekends.

BLEARY: Ten minutes? How do you give it a good read?

HAGGARD: After a while, most of them won't even take five. The point is to get them done. Period. Sure you'll blow a couple; that's expected. But there are checks and balances along the way in the system. Even so, occasionally a kid falls through the cracks. Can't be helped. Things happen fast. They have to.

BLEARY: I *was* a little blown away by the speed of the early-action decisions in committee. I mean, boom boom boom, most kids took no more than two minutes.

HAGGARD *(shakes his head):* Oh boy. Wait'll regular committee starts in February. Two minutes is an eternity. The December meetings are like stop-action slow motion compared to March. Last year we made four hundred forty-four decisions in *one day* between ten o'clock and four—and we broke for lunch for half an hour! Of course, those were New Jersey applicants, so it doesn't really count.

BLEARY *(laughing):* Hey, be careful, I'm from New Jersey.

HAGGARD: I knew there was something weird about you. But we see so many apps from there that we go to committee with them specially prepped for speed. We took—what?—twenty-four percent of our applicants overall last year; you know what the New Jersey percentage was?

BLEARY: Something like nineteen, wasn't it?

HAGGARD: Fifteen. Fifteen percent! The alumni out there almost shed their skins over that. But listen, that's true—about the lower ratio, I mean—in every area where we get a ton of apps.

BLEARY: It won't be much better this year if the kids I'm seeing are any indication. I don't know why, but the last few days have been full of essays on dying pets by the pom-pom crowd. And I've still got a bunch to go. Speaking of which . . .

HAGGARD: Yeah, yeah. Read. *(They return to their folders, leafing through the forms, writing short paragraphs of evaluation, and occasionally shaking their heads over an application. Sarah sips at her coffee, Henry quaffs from his beer. He starts on the second bottle.)*

BLEARY: Listen to this one.

HAGGARD: I warn you, what you're about to do constitutes assault with a deadly weapon in some states.

BLEARY *(reading from the essay):* "I, Bradley T. Borewell, am a happy, well-rounded student. Through hard work and much study I have been able to produce this result."

HAGGARD *(sighting down the barrel of an imaginary rifle):* Bang. It was self-defense, Your Honor.

BLEARY *(yawning and stretching):* I think today's exercise in sadomasochism is over.

HAGGARD: Going so soon?

BLEARY *(getting up and looking at the kitchen clock):* It's almost midnight. There're still some left, but as you would say, what's tomorrow for, right? *(She goes to the closet for her coat and piles her folders into a canvas bag of her own.)*

HAGGARD: If it weren't so late that it will be early soon, I might ask what you're doing later. I might ask you anyway.

BLEARY: Very amusing, Henry.

HAGGARD: Admissions officers are people too, you know.

BLEARY: Doesn't feel like it. I feel like a folder-reading marionette. Wind me up and I do forty a day.

HAGGARD: If you're lucky.

BLEARY: See you tomorrow. Thanks for the coffee. And the wild times. *(She moves toward the door. Still on the couch, he twists and stretches out his arms in mock panic.)*

HAGGARD: No no, don't leave me here alone with *them!*

(But she is gone. Henry slumps back and looks at his pile.)

HAGGARD: Five more. But first . . .

(He goes into the kitchen and returns with another beer. Settling on the couch, his eyes half-lidded, he picks up the next folder, his thirty-eighth of the day—YOUR APPLICATION.)

Fadeout, with the sound of snoring in the background.

WHAT IT MEANS

This is your audience. Study them well. Not exactly the Nobel Prize panel. There are other members of the committee, of course, each of them different, but Henry and Sarah are types that predominate. There are actually two basic species of admissions officer—the Temps *(miserabilis overworkus)* and the Lifers *(cynica terminus)*. The Temps are likely to be young, enthusiastic, and often recently graduated from the school they're working for. They're intelligent but not usually bookish, and hired largely for their sales appeal; the wholesome type abounds among young admissions officers.

Temps are interested in using admissions work as an interesting time-killer until they enter graduate school or business or, now and then, college academics. A few end up in high schools as teachers and guidance counselors. Henry Haggard and Sarah Bleary are Temps.

Lifers, on the other hand, at the top level, are the big guns who set policy and run the show. Just below that is a class of itinerant admissions soldiers, Lifers all, who move from school to school, slowly climbing the ladder toward a directorship somewhere. Many of them began, in their salad days, as Temps, but got caught up in the business through inclination or inertia. No one ever prepares to be a Lifer—it just happens. Some are hard-core bureaucrats, and some have fallen into a comfortable career from more precarious faculty jobs. (Tenured professorships—the only secure college teaching appointments—are difficult to get.) Admissions offers lots of benefits—reasonable job security, free tuition for family members, good vacations, and in most cases a lovely and lively place to live.

Lifers can range from the increasingly rare old-boy type (craggy brow, football- and hockey-crazy, green pants with snowflake pattern, watches golf on TV) to the dynamic young computer-oriented management breed now beginning to multiply in the business. It is, essentially, a young person's field. As Henry Haggard suggested, there's too much burnout. Lifers don't read as many folders as Temps, though they do wield more weight in policy.

(This seems as good a place as any to mention the obvious: Incompetence occurs as frequently in admissions offices as it does elsewhere, which is to say, with discouraging semiregularity. There's not much you can do about this, but it might soften the blow if you're rejected. "They wouldn't know something good if it hit them in the face," you can say. But, like umpires who may now and then blow a call, admissions offices are not known for changing their decisions.)

Both Temps and Lifers are great at parties. They are outgoing and charming, professional interviewers and minglers and smilers. Somewhere underneath it all, in most cases, is some legitimate interest in education or in kids, but between the superficial smiles and the deeper sympathy grows a very stubborn layer of cynicism. It blisters rapidly into callus, even in the newest recruits. These are your readers.

WHO DECIDES?

The Temps and the early Lifers do the bulk of the application reading. In fact, at some of the most competitive colleges, the admissions office hires outside readers, from graduate students to deans' spouses, to pick up the slack. The more seniority you have, the fewer folders you read. It's understandable. Folder reading is the drudge work, and directors want to look at the big picture. The irony is that the readers have less to say about policy but more about individual decisions—more therefore about your application, especially if you're in the Gray Area.

FIRST AND SECOND READING

Most folders are read twice. Henry and Sarah are in stage one. Theirs are the first comments to darken your file. (They also rate you *numerically* as a student and as a person, usually on a scale from one to five or six.) Colleges handle first reading differently. At Brown, applications are first-read at random; only later does the admissions officer covering your geographical area, the person who is going to present you to the committee—and essentially make the decision on you—read your application. At Columbia, on the other hand, folders are first-read by the officer in charge of your area and second-read randomly by faculty, grad students, and anyone else the admissions office can corral to help ease the load.

At some colleges, though—Harvard and Princeton among them—every folder doesn't even get to the director. Applicants are screened by a few readers in a "regional committee." Admissions officers will tell you that only the obvious rejects don't make that first cut, but built into such a system is great pressure to trim the workload of the director's final committee and to *save time.* You can bet that almost everyone who's weeded out early belongs to Just Folks.

At all the colleges, it is the reading of the *area person* that counts most—the second reader in a process like Brown's, the first in one like Columbia's. The area officer looks at you in relation to other applicants from your school and your region. The area person literally "knows where you're coming from."

RIFFRAFF READERS

Faculty

You are not writing for a panel of professors. Although at smaller colleges a faculty member or two may be more involved in admissions—they may even be given time off to work in the office—decisions are made overwhelmingly by Temps and Lifers. Admissions officers wish it were not so, but faculty at schools like the Ivy colleges are not typically concerned with the admissions operation, except to howl occasionally that the freshmen in their classes can't write English. The last thing professors want to do is read twenty folders a day.

Hired Guns

Many colleges employ part-time readers to trim the folder population. These may include anyone from graduate students to the dean's relatives by marriage. Hired-gun readings are often wild cards. They do not share the embattled admissions office psyche, and so they sometimes read the folders more carefully (because they read only a few). They have quirkier tastes. But the subtleties of grades and schools are a code they only dimly understand; the hired gun therefore almost always leans heavily on the essay, a document everyone understands, and which speaks (you hope) plainly in your favor.

THE COMMITTEE MEETING

By the time your application gets to the "full" admissions committee—usually the director, the presenter, and one or two other officers (everybody else is busy reading folders)—the decision is made. Very rarely does the committee overturn the presenter's recommendations, and such reversals often involve an applicant from one of the Lobby groups. In fact, in the case of an experienced Temp who has established credibility, the committee is likely to be just a rubber stamp.

SCENE: A richly appointed old room in the admissions building at First Choice, with dark wood paneling, a wood and marble fireplace, and recessed mahogany bookshelves. On the walls are original prints of First Choice as it looked in colonial times. In the center of the room, in high-backed chairs around a massive antique oval table polished to a high gloss, sit Henry Haggard, today's presenter; at his left, the director; and across from Haggard, Sarah Bleary—the "committee." Beside Haggard is an im-

mense tray bulging with folders. On the floor next to the director, three more trays—admit, reject, wait list—await the cascade of folders soon to begin. Before each officer is a thick computer printout, the "docket" of all applicants, which shows SATs, class rank, and other numerical information, as well as the one-to-five ratings given by admissions readers. Against one wall is a bulletin board covered with outlandish pictures applicants have sent in of themselves.

DIRECTOR: What've you got?

HAGGARD: Twelve Admits, ninety-seven Rejects, three Wait List. And one great pic for the board.

DIRECTOR: You're tough.

HAGGARD: We're talking about the Bronx, here.

DIRECTOR: OK. Shoot.

HAGGARD *(hands director his first file; director flips through it):* Bronx Polytech first. Black girl with good numbers, no dad, oldest of four, all brothers, mom's a nurse, easy A. *(As he will do for every folder, the director marks it with a special pen and and puts it in the proper bin. He takes the next folder from Haggard.)* Another easy one, astro numbers but not a nerd, works part-time with the homeless, teachers ecstatic, two varsity sports—nothing special, but still—and a great essay about his best friend—

DIRECTOR: OK.

HAGGARD: Next one's not so easy, but a good one, I think. Some spark here.

DIRECTOR: Readers are high for a kid with those numbers.

HAGGARD: Grades are solid in a decent program, but check out the essay. "I do some of my best thinking in the bathroom," it starts. [See p. 119.]

DIRECTOR *(glancing at it):* C'mon.

HAGGARD: Yup. But he plays it out really well—funny, thoughtful, really sharp. You don't see many like this. Here's the kid you want in your class.

DIRECTOR: If he doesn't spend all his time in the john. *(Director writes "A" on the folder.)* Who's next?

HAGGARD: Next one I wanted you to see before we hang him out to dry.

DIRECTOR: Wait list? Those stats are awfully good compared to the Bathroom Buddha.

HAGGARD: Pre-med and flat as a pancake personally. Unbelievably dumb essay, school just repeats the obvious about math-science ability, and teachers don't really know him. Does zippo.

BLEARY: This the kid I read?

HAGGARD: Yup.

BLEARY: The essay's all about how working with microbes made him a better person. He's deadly.

HAGGARD: His dad's some kind of research doctor, that's how he got the lab job.

DIRECTOR: Why not an R? What's keeping him in? You're saying he doesn't offer us a thing.

HAGGARD: I'd be for an R but the school would go nuts. Because that's all we're—

DIRECTOR *(looking down at his docket):* That's it at old Bronx Poly? Nineteen rejects?

HAGGARD: That's right.

DIRECTOR *(writing WL on the first and then R's on a pile of folders):* I don't want to hear from them on this.

HAGGARD: I'll take care of it. They've got a pretty good idea what's coming. It was a weak class.

DIRECTOR: Next.

HAGGARD: Minuet High . . .

Get the idea? The director doesn't even have *time* to read the essay. He sees the beginning, perhaps, and skims the rest. The director wants to spend the minimum amount of time on a case, so the other admissions officers read the essay *for* him, in effect. The readers make the difference.

Let's look in some detail at the ways applicants unwittingly make all this speed possible.

3 Danger: Sleepy Prose Ahead (or, The Sandman Cometh)

Now you've gotten a glimpse of the road your application will travel and had a peek at your reading audience. You've seen the piles of folders that fill up their houses and their lives like big clumps of fallen leaves over a sewer, a blockage that naturally begins to affect the flow of minor details like eating and sleeping. You know that when they're poring bug-eyed over twenty or thirty or forty applications a day, they're liable to let sleeping essays lie. And *your* application may be in that stack—it may be number thirty-eight. Your first job, then, is this: prevent them from falling asleep.

Go back to the writer's questions: What kind of piece is it? The word essay comes from the French word that means "attempt." It's a short piece not intended to exhaust the subject—or the reader. Even among essays, the college essay is a form all its own, with conventions and clichés that admissions officers like Henry Haggard, lying catatonic at midnight on couches all across the country, know only too well. You, as a practitioner of the form, should know them too, and steer clear. (Admissions officers may be tired, but it's hardly your responsibility to *help* them catch up on sleep.) Let's rummage into Henry Haggard's bag for some of the most common snooze potions whipped up by seniors. We don't have to dig very deep:

*1. The Trip.*This is the one about the visit to Europe, Israel, Kansas, or other exotic land. Applicants make The Trip in the company of family, peers, or even alone in one of the many programs that take students into the home of a foreign family to live. But wherever they are, 99 percent of the travelers seem determined to ignore the small and homely (but significant) details around them in favor of sweeping banalities: "I had to adjust to a whole new way of life. The first thing I noticed was the food, which was very different, as were all the customs; my adopted family's habits were quite different from anything I was used to, but, by the end of my stay, I had come to accept them. I realized that neither I nor they were wrong, but simply different." These essays, as you may be able to guess by now, are *not* very different. It seems that all writers of The Trip "eventually got used to all the cultural differences" and "finally felt like part of the family." But where are the colors and textures and flavors of something seen and experienced fresh?

These travels, of course, "broadened my horizons" and "gave me a new perspective on my native land, the United States." Often, applicants report that living in a foreign country, whose language they had been studying in school, "increased my fluency and facility immensely." Surprise!

Also well trampled are the Trip paths leading to vague forms of self-discovery in far-flung ancestral homelands. "I got a very religious feeling from the Sistine Chapel and I was proud to be an Italian." These essays usually show the strong influence of the brochures and airplane travel magazines from which they were lifted. At the end of the Ancestral Trip, writers swell with pride and platitudes at having "learned more than I ever could in history class about my cultural heritage."

Even wilderness trips, like Outward Bound, can somehow get boiled down into this soggy formula. "On my trip to the Grand Tetons, I learned to work with people and stretch my abilities to the utmost." Change the first phrase to "In my work as a terrorist," and the sentiment still holds.

2. *My Favorite Things.*This "list" essay (most lists are bad) is usually written in a hand which dots its *i*'s with little circles and often takes off from an opening something like, "Things I am for: puppy dogs, freedom, big soft pillows, and Mrs. Field's cookies. Things I am against: nuclear war, pimples, racial discrimination, spinach." Written by males and females alike, it is the unmistakable sign of what is called, in admissions lingo, the Fluffball.

3. Miss America. The Big Issue questions, like "Please comment on an issue of national or international concern," lead a lot of people into this trap. "I think World Peace is the most important issue facing us today . . ." and so on like a beauty queen. Equally flimsy stuff pops up about almost any front-page issue— apartheid, Nicaragua, nukes.

At best these pieces sound like the small-town editorials of outraged old ladies. The arguments, no matter how powerfully right you feel, no matter how seriously you study the topic in school or debate it across the dinner table, are plagiaristic and generic. Admissions committees do not want to know how slavishly you can regurgitate views of parents, teachers, or national news magazines.

4. Jock. This is not a topic as much as a whole way of thinking, so it is certainly not confined to essays by big-necked boys who breathe through their mouths. It seems to have spread like mildew into writing on every activity students pursue and is by far the most common approach among earnest and intelligent students trying too hard to impress an admissions committee. Musicians, actors, lab interns, yearbook editors, club officers— students from every walk of high school life have succumbed to the questionable charms of the Jock essay, flocking like doomed ducks to a wooden decoy. Still, though, scholar-athletes sound its most familiar and resonant note: "Through wrestling I have learned to set goals, to go all out, and to work with people." Now *that's* a frightening prospect.

Anyone can (and too many do) fill in this formula: Through *blank* (piano playing, spider collecting, touch typing) I have learned Noble Value A, High Platitude B, and Great Lesson C. The result affects an admissions officer like Valium and doesn't show anything about you, except that you may have succeeded in spending seventeen happy, thought-free years.

5. My Room.A common variation on number two. "I don't know what to tell you about myself, so I guess I'll describe my room. That just about says it all." This opening is followed by a highlighted tour up and down the room's Himalayas of records, baseball gloves, and miscellaneous junk, accompanied by some self-conscious (and very old) jokes about messes and cleanliness: "Anyway, a clean desk is the sign of an empty mind." So is this essay.

6. Three D's. Another recipe that tries to tell readers what to think of you. "I honestly believe that I have the *d*iscipline and *d*etermination and *d*iversity of interests to succeed at whatever I do." Maybe. But probably not at the college that receives an essay beginning with that line, because those three D's equal one more: *dull.*

7. Tales of My Success (or, The Time I Won My Town the Race).A particularly deadly Jock/Three D combination. "But, finally, when I crossed the finish line first and received the congratulations of my teammates, I realized all the hard work had been worth it." Why must all stories of sports, elections, and other "challenges" (there's another cliché for you) end on a note of Napoleonic triumph? Or, if not triumph, then the righteous tone of the principled crusader who stood for what was right but, alas, went down to defeat.

8. Pet Death. Maudlin descriptions of animal demise, always written by the Fluffball. "As I watched Buttons's life ebb away, I came to value the important things in this world."

9. Selling and Telling—Autobiography. Trying to say anything meaningful about a whole life in five hundred words can reduce any writer to absurdity. But if your essay begins, "Hello, my name is . . ." your application is going into the pile with the old potato chips. If you've gotten anything out of this book so far, you probably won't make such a simple gaffe, though every year a surprising number of perfectly capable students do.

Most of the other autobiographical strategies are only slightly better. "I am a very unique person with many interests and abilities and goals," is one dreary classic. Would *you* want to read three hundred of those?

The Family Salute is another. "I come from a close-knit

family. I have a very close relationship with my parents and siblings"—not sisters and brothers, notice—"and my eighty-three-year-old grandmother and I are especially close." The writer's parents may have been close for years (once, at least, they were *very* close) and are probably standing close behind her as she writes her essay. But admissions officers do not get close to the writer, her eyes and ears and mind and heart.

One more word about the pitfalls of the autobiography. I knew an admissions officer who used to pick up his pencil when he noticed too many sentences beginning with a capital *I*. Then he'd start circling them. When the total number of circles got too high for him to bear, he simply recommended a reject and went on to the next file.

Henry Haggards nationwide are snoring like polar bears over all these essays because students writing them are still asking, "What do they want on those college essays?" The point is, you can't force the committee into liking you. You can't tell them what to think. Admissions officers are unusually well equipped with a device Ernest Hemingway prescribed for writers: "a built-in shock-proof shit detector." They're awfully hard to snow with strategies of any kind—no one hates the hard sell more than an admissions officer.

By now, you may be thinking I've blown all your ideas out of the water. Hang on. There are ways to get them to like you without a lot of advertising talk and salesmanship, without assigning yourself a sampling of virtues you think sound good, without empty take-no-chances rhetoric. In fact, getting rid of all those things improves your prospects immediately.

How do you do it? What's left to write about?

Everything.

WRITING

4 Chilling Out

Consider the following opening of an essay, which seems at first to be a typical "Hello" autobiography.

> I was born on October 22, 1960. There is nothing remarkable about this except that I spent the Sixties in a state of semiconsciousness and missed out on the Beatles. These days, though, a beginning like that seems somehow depressing, and I am not consoled by the fact that there were probably millions of others who had the misfortune to be born at the tail end of the baby boom. I don't think I can ever forgive my parents for not acting sooner.

There is authority and humor here, and awareness. He realizes that his opening is ordinary, and he plays on it surprisingly in the second line by showing that he knows it's banal; at the same time he begins to see some meaning in something as simple as his birthdate. We realize, in fact, that he was setting us up with that first line. We're having fun, suddenly. It's as if we are hiking through a wilderness with an expert outdoorsman; none of us is quite sure where the next step will be, but we have confidence the journey will be worthwhile. The sound is fresh. The turns of thought are surprising. We are hearing a *voice*. The joke at the end brings more than a smile—it steers a reader to the point of the essay: why being born in 1960 was such a big deal. Let's listen to the answer.

> Most of my generation (at least this is what *US News and World Report* tells me) lament that by the time we became

pubescent we were merely stranded in the wake of something big that had happened. None of us, certainly not I, knew at first what we had missed, but the realization that our generation would be only a few lines in The American Pageant while our older brothers and sisters would be appended and multi-footnoted hit me like the first blast of winter. It seemed, when this moment of consciousness came, that there was nothing left to do in a worn-out world. Everything that should have been done or tried had been done or tried. A large portion of it had failed, which only decreased the probability that it would be attempted again in my time. All that the *real* children of the Sixties could do was play records made by people and organizations no longer in the papers. When my world view came of its own (that is, when I was allowed to cross a two-way street by myself) I saw behind me a decade that couldn't be matched and ahead of me a generation that wasn't about to try. Knowing that my life was effectively doomed to dullness somewhat lessened the impact of the axiom that each day should be a new learning experience. What was so new? All I had to do to find out anything important was ask a twenty-one-year-old or read old copies of *Life*. I could, of course, wait for the next revolution. Ideally, I could start another, but the disease which I so readily diagnosed in others applied to me just as well. I didn't really care; it was much easier to fantasize. The idea that the Sagging Seventies were made to be played out with every part prewritten in the style of *As The World Turns*, with neither interest nor importance of action, had solidified in my mind, and in the words of Arlo Guthrie, "There was a-nothing I could do about it."

But also I knew there must be something more than the fact of late arrival, something within my peers and me which put us in our state. As I look around at the classes of '78, I can see little or nothing of passionate commitment. I perceive no idealism, no hate, no guilt, and no audacity. All I can see is thousands of would-be doctors and lawyers who want nothing more than to live in Garden City. For me, their goal leads to erosion of the soul and higher property taxes. I mean, I know I'm seventeen and think that I'm going to live forever and I really should plan for the year

1989, but the idea that my generation will become the Era of Public Accountancy is frightening. I don't want my friends to clean up after the last mess; I want us to make our own.

In my analysis of what everything would be like should the UN suddenly decide to make me king of the world, I don't want riots in the streets or pillaging. I want intelligence of purpose rather than a prefabricated existence. The Seventies are not over yet, and where people are concerned—even where I am concerned—there is always hope. Wherever I go to college, I want least of all to see and be part of the continuation of the Null Generation. I want us to be just as much a part of history as our older brothers and sisters.

Maybe finishing out the decade won't be so bad after all. I mean, I can always go to see *Beatlemania*.

NO BAD TOPICS

But, you say, that essay falls right into the forbidden modes—it could be either the Autobiography or the Big Issue. Relax. Contradiction Number One: There are no good or bad topics for college essays, only good or bad essays. John Updike said, "There is a great deal to be said about almost anything. Everything can be as interesting as every other thing." Sometimes good writing is just the result of reinvigorating what has become a mundane cliché. In your essay, you don't have to say something startling and new, or strain to be "different." The writer above doesn't make any contributions to the store of human knowledge. He just says what he knows in a fresh way that allows us to *see for ourselves* who he is.

This doesn't diminish the danger in all the deadly essays in chapter three, but now that you know the traps of the Nerdly Nine, you are ready to understand that most of them—Big Issue, Trip, Autobiography, even Pet Death—can be lively and revealing. Even the old second-grade standby, My Summer Vacation, can lead to excellent writing (see chapter twelve, "Summer Beyond Wish").

In fact, one student, after hearing my litany of traps for the unwary, wrote this:

> Recently, I spent a day being told that my life is one big cliché. The assembly that morning concerned the writing of the college essay, and the speaker, a former Horace Mann English teacher, proceeded to explain to a once-eager-but-then-doubt-riddled teenage crowd why every essay topic they had ever conceived was taboo. We couldn't write about our summer trip, our dedication to extracurriculars, our views on world issues—in essence, our life up until now, because it has all been *done* before; the admissions officer, upon reading our humble compositions, will let out a long wail from beneath his pile of boring, clichéd essays, toss said humble compositions in the corner, and drown himself in Heineken. Hm.
>
> Later that day, someone told me about a theory that there are only twelve stories in the world, and that every story I hear or tell is a variation of one of those twelve, thus eliminating any possibility that I could write something you haven't seen before once every twelve applications. Oh.
>
> In my Dostoevsky class, we discussed Raskolnikov's fear that life means absolutely nothing unless you are Napoleon or some other person that everybody keeps talking about. In other words, unless you kill a lot of people or discover another element, you have to resign yourself to a life full of rush-hour traffic and bank deposits and take-out Chinese food and tax returns and sitcoms and other things that are ridiculous just because everyone does them. Yes, yes, that's so true, concurred my English class. Ugh.
>
> Ladies and gentlemen of the admissions committee, I have a dilemma. I have been told that my life is one big cliché, and I don't believe that's true. But how can I express this to you? How can I get you to say "yes, Miss Sharon Isaak, we want you to come to Princeton, you are a wonderful example of a non-cliché and we want you to come add your non-clichéness to our academic community"? I don't think I can accomplish my task in the frenzied atmosphere of this ominous piece of paper. No, ladies and gentlemen, I think I shall invite you to dinner, and we shall see what happens from there.
>
> Let's make it a Sunday; Sundays are good because they

give you a whole weekend to recuperate from the all nighters you pulled the week before (you while reading essays, I while writing them). No need to dress up, though you'll want to wear sweaters because dinner will be outside, on a wooden table underneath a tree. I think each of us should bring a part of the meal, to put some personality into it. I will be bringing guacamole, of which I'm quite fond, so make your selections accordingly.

Once we eat, we can start talking about ourselves. I'm sure that after a good meal of guacamole and whatever, we'll be able to get beyond the problem of the cliché'd existence, for I know that there's more behind the title "we as admissions officers," as I'm sure you know there's more behind my green and gray résumé. I'll tell you some stories, like the one about the time some friends and I baked chocolate chip cookies on an iron propped between a pair of sneakers at Exeter Summer School or about the game of strip poker I won because I was wearing a lot of jewelry, leaving the editor of my school newspaper in his long underwear during a 40-degree-below-zero frostwave. By the time we have dessert and coffee I'm sure you'll see that though the world would love to include my life in the long list of already-been-dones (and no matter what I say, the world will always try to do so), I'm much more fun to spend time with than your run-of-the-mill, self-conscious statistic. Hey, the things I do are new when I do them, aren't they? Thinking that way sure makes life a lot more fun than spending a lifetime as a generalization.

Anyway, I look forward to your visit. (R.S.V.P. by December 15.)

Admissions officers usually hate essays about application anxieties, but this one so charmed a reader that he sent a note of appreciation to Sharon. She just reacted to what was happening around her. You can make a college essay out of *anything;* the materials are everywhere.

GETTING READY TO WRITE

Approach is everything. Here are some ideas to keep in mind as you begin.

1. If you ask what "they" are looking for, you are already on the wrong track. What do *you* have to say? That's what they want to hear. Many of the applications themselves tell you to write about "anything you want." Take them at their word. If the thing that intrigues you most lately is that your seven-year-old sister is the one person in the house who can get the VCR to work, write about that, not World Peace; you have the beginnings of a good Big Issue essay.

2. Find a reader, or readers. Friends, brothers or sisters, pen pals, maybe a teacher you know and trust; *someone* who will respond to your writing in the right spirit. I can't emphasize this enough. You are writing for readers now, and you need to train yourself to say something worth reading. They should simply be people who like good writing and can read your work without preconceived notions about what it should say. They have to be honest, and they have to care about you. It is often mutually inspiring to have your reader(s) also applying to college. You can swap ideas and frustrations. One warning about parents, though. They may want you to "sell yourself," an approach that is dead wrong. One of my former students, now at Harvard, looks back on this experience:

> Acting as my own counselor: I have a vision of my parents standing outside my bedroom door, listening for the sound of Pencil on Paper, waiting with all that bated breath for the definitive article, that damn college essay. My father tried to tell me how to write it:
> "They don't even read your application, so stop wasting so much time on it!"
> "How do you know? Mr. Bauld says we should treat it like our first piece of published writing."
> "So fine. So give them something that will show them how terrific you are. Your mother and I think you're terrific, and you trust our opinions, so tell them how great you are."

Parents have their uses, but reading your college essay isn't usually one of them. They care too much, and often don't know quite enough.

3. Write something only you could write. It should have a sound as distinctive as your speaking voice. The problem with most essays is that they could have been written by anyone. In one sense, your writing "voice" is simply a polished version of your speech; but remember how that speech changes when you're talking to different audiences, like teachers or friends. It's the same you, but your word choice, tone, sentence rhythms, and even the sound of your voice change. Just as you speak in a different "voice" to parents and friends, so you must find the one that's right for this purpose. The voice you should be aiming at is one you'd use toward an acquaintance you wanted to be better friends with. (Remember, admissions officers already know you when they read your essay.) Though it's not the voice you'd use with your *best* friend, it's not formal, either. Don't write as a kid trying to impress an adult, in what you imagine is an "educated" voice. You have two or three different voices of your own, and you should explore and use them. A good essay is like an interesting letter from someone you once met.

4. Know what you write about. This is a slight twist on the common writing advice, "Write about what you know." The professional writers in chapter twelve know a lot—everything from history and foreign languages to the design of playing cards. That's part of the reason their writing is good. But be comforted. Writing is discovery—writers often don't realize what they know about something until they try to discuss it in print. If you find you don't know anything well enough to write about it thoughtfully or entertainingly, you've learned something disturbing but not irreversible. And you're wrong—you know more than enough. Think of yourself as a reporter working on a story, the subject of which happens to be your own life and interests. Your memory is your file drawer, and in that file are your research materials. You're looking for *significant details*. These appear in the humblest and most ordinary things you do every day, usually in a more interesting way than they do in the Big Moments (being elected student body president, or scoring the winning water polo goal), those events in which so many college essayists try unsuccessfully to find Meaning. Instead, how about paying attention to that pigeon on your windowsill and what you eat for lunch—and why. If the unexamined life is not worth living, it's certainly not worth writing about.

5. A college essay is an informal, or familiar, piece. All the questions, even the Big Issues, are really asking for some kind of personal statement. Don't even think of it as school-related writing. It is not a history or English paper. Loosen up. You are after the most natural tone and style possible—a kind of inspired conversation, scrubbed clean of all its hesitations, repetitions, and vagueness. It is as personal as a phone call.

6. Entertain. I don't mean you have to sound like Rodney Dangerfield. But all writing entertains at some level. "Entertainment" has gotten a bad name over the years, a reputation as a lightweight; people say, "It isn't a very thought-provoking movie; it's pure entertainment." As if only things that turn your mind into fruit punch are entertaining! To truly entertain doesn't mean to open with a few lame jokes, or to sink everything to the level of TV sitcom. It means to sustain a voice worth listening to. You can be as serious or as frivolous as you like, whatever suits you. But when you write, write to give pleasure to your audience. You'll write a more impressive essay than if you set out only to impress.

A WORD ABOUT HUMOR

You'll hear a great deal of conflicting advice about humor. Counselors, teachers, and parents often talk about humor as if it should (and could) be confined like a noisy chicken, occasionally let out for a good squawking and then locked up again in its dingy coop while we get on with really important business. "Oh, humor has its place," they may say, "but not in your college essay." Or, "If you must joke, don't try to be *too* funny," they warn. "You can't be sure admissions officers share your idea of what's funny."

Wrong.

Nothing very good was ever written by someone afraid to say something funny. An enormous portion of the writing that has outlived its author—what the world calls literature—has humor in its heart. Shakespeare's darkest tragedies also include his funniest writing. Even the Bible is not above a little risqué slapstick (Genesis 31:32–35, for instance). What your advisers may have in their own hearts is the fear that not everyone can pull it off. That's true. But here is another truth: Humor is a virtue, part of what it means to be human. (Of course, the same can be said for sincerity.) What to do? The following rule will guide you infallibly: If you think of something funny about your topic, write it down. If you don't, don't.

It's that simple. Trouble arises when an applicant thinks he *should* write something funny or clever to be "different" and then grunts out a noisy and jangling piece that doesn't communicate but calls attention to itself, like a broken toy. Trouble also arises when an applicant thinks he *should* write something solemn or serious to be "safe," and carefully extracts every trace of living tissue from an essay like some ghoulish literary surgeon. What your advisers may not understand is that funny is not the opposite of sincere. "Funny," wrote G.K. Chesterton, a very funny essayist, "is the opposite of not funny, and of nothing else." If you see things in a funny way, everything you write will be funny. You can't help it. It's part of you, of your voice.

Admissions officers, like any other readers, are suspicious of something that shows *no* sense of humor. Your essay should show the way you deal with the world every day; though writing can't let someone hear your laugh, your essay should at least hint that you have one.

5 Warming Up

The hardest thing to do is budge an object from a dead start, particularly if that object is your brain. Once you're in motion, momentum takes over, but sometimes just grunting out those first sentences takes all your strength.

How do you get going? Turn Off the Self-Criticism. Many people, when they begin to write, stop after the first line. "That isn't what I meant," they say, and fuss with a word or phrase. Meanwhile, a big blank page still waits. The temptation to edit before you write is strong, but you can train yourself to resist it. The rewards will be great if you do. Write now, revise later. They are separate steps in the process.

Never outline. Writing outlines at the beginning is like writing postcards home describing the scenery *before* you go on the trip. If you haven't been there yet, how do you know what it's going to be like? There may come a time, after you have written and rewritten, when an outline may help you organize your materials. But first you need some materials to organize.

In the early stages, write everything *fast,* without stopping. Don't worry about coherence yet, or about where to start—just get your thoughts out in whatever crazy pattern they occur. Start anywhere. That's what professional writers do. Certainly don't worry about mechanics or correctness; you'll make cuts and additions later. This is just stage one. Good writing doesn't spring from people perfect and complete, like Athena from the forehead of Zeus. You'll need to make at least a few drafts to get it in shape. How long that takes varies from writer to writer. You'll get to know your own working schedule, but figure on roughly a few days per essay—at least.

WHAT DO I HAVE TO SAY?

The answer, of course, is *plenty*. The first step is learning to recognize what you already know and experience every day, and to see it with new eyes. It is not an exaggeration to say that every day you gather material for another college essay.

THE NOTEBOOK

Keep a notebook of ideas and observations, pieces of conversation and events, and write something in it every day. Keep to a minimum the diary diarrhea: "Saw *her* today. She does not know I exist. She's still going out with that dope," etc. Instead, an essay writer's notebook is a quarry filled with more substantial nuggets that find their way into polished pieces later:

> Everything a big bore today. Sat in back row in French. Mr. J's voice like faraway buzzing of bees. Feels good to be almost asleep in class, like a velvet curtain about to come down. Danger, though.
>
> * * *
>
> Went to a Mostly Mozart concert last night. Music the usual tinkling. Tiptoe stuff. Good exposure to culture, Mom says. I read somewhere a lot of people die of exposure each year, and I hope I'm not one of them. Slumped over my seat when the lights are turned up. But the hour before the concert is great, sitting on the fountain outside, the sun already gone but still light out. It's cool, and everybody's out, nobody pushing or shoving, just drifting. No rush. Everybody looks lighter.
>
> * * *
>
> Someone sent me a chain letter! Fantastic. I don't quite get it, though—something about a South American priest who started it, and it's full of examples of what happens if you don't send it out to twenty friends. Some guy made a million dollars and then lost it the next day and

jumped off a building, great stories like that. I wish I had it here. If I send it out I'll be rich soon, it said. Who thinks these things up?

It also teems with fragments that may go nowhere, though at the time they were written they struck a resonant chord:

> There were two pigeons on the wall around lunch, one chasing, fluffing up his neck like they do, the other running away. Probably male and female, the old hot pursuit. Typical.

A notebook is a gathering of acorns against an uninspired winter. You may want to show some parts of your notebook to your readers; the material in it can eventually form the backbone of your college essay. It is especially useful as a warm-up before you begin to write something else, but when you get in the habit you'll find yourself making notes at all hours, scribbling away on napkins, bits of newspaper, and other scraps; your muse may not wait for you to sit down at your desk with your Cross pen, but may attack on the bus on the way home, with only an ice cream wrapper handy. An oft-repeated story about Kurt Vonnegut, the novelist, has him beginning his day at work by describing in detail something he saw or experienced that morning, even if only what he had for breakfast, the colors and tastes of something observed; like an appetizer, it gets the juices going.

Your notebook can be a good sounding board for the different voices you want to experiment with. Try imitating other writers. Write as if you were indeed writing to *her* (or *him*). What would you say? (No schmaltz.) Write down all your dreams. Write a full news story of your first memory. (See Mencken, p. 132.) If you need more detail for such a story, do what a reporter would do—interview the other witnesses, like your parents, to flesh out the incident. Tell the whole story of your first school day or your first-grade year. Write dialogue: a) conversations you had or b) conversations you overheard. Describe your best friend to your worst enemy.

This is your substitute for outlining. Writing is traveling through uncharted territory—your mind. You are the first traveler, and your essays are the world's first maps. So you can't know in advance where you're going. That doesn't mean you don't have a *direction*. But sometimes the direction is marked only by a few big landmarks you can see from where you stand, and taken down in a shorthand like this:

> 1st dance cl. downtown—HUGE studio, big pipes in the ceiling. My pink warmers, ratty jazz shoes, torn sweatshirt OK. Everybody staring, checking out, is she real? Instr.—dark complexion, high cheekbones—goddess in plastic pants.

There's a difference between note-taking and indiscriminate scribbling. Make sure, in your note-taking, that you fill in enough of the sights and sounds and ideas to allow you to recapture your thoughts and see the images when you reread the entry. Remember, you may be reading it long afterward. Whenever you can, make sentences.

To find good material for a college essay in your daily life, learn to notice the sometimes small surprises that interrupt the dull procession of yesterdays that threaten to consume all our lives. It's a common observation that most people spend their lives focused on the ground just ahead, unaware of the startling details all around them. But fiction sometimes pales in comparison to what's true. "If men would steadily observe realities only," wrote Henry David Thoreau, "and not allow themselves to be deluded, life, to compare it with such things as we know, would be like a fairy tale and the Arabian Nights' Entertainments." Sometimes to write, all you have to do is open your eyes.

STRANGER THAN FICTION

Use your notebook to teach yourself to see. A diary is the record of routine, but the notebook of an essay writer is filled with truths that are Stranger than Fiction. These are the intersections where the remarkable and the ordinary cross paths for a moment. For instance, at the school where I taught we had a guitar teacher named Strum, a swimming coach named Kramp, and an English

teacher named Reid. Not to mention a bald teacher named Bauld.
All perfect notebook fodder.

Here are some Stranger than Fiction entries from different
notebooks:

> Two bums on 104th St. near Broadway, leaning
> against a stoop, arguing over whether Thunderbird or Colt
> 45 is better. Like connoisseurs. "That stuff too *heavy*, I don't
> deal with that."
>
> * * *
>
> There's a guy every week who plays an upright piano
> under the arch in Washington Square Park. It has bright
> green keys and all the guts of it are exposed. When he
> finishes, he rolls it away over the cement.
>
> * * *
>
> At the beach we saw a woman with a tattoo on her
> shoulder in the shape of a butterfly.
>
> * * *
>
> I saw a horse galloping down the middle of the road,
> without saddle or rider and with reins hanging from his
> chin. He turned a corner and came head to head with an
> oncoming car and both braked to a stop, the horse and car
> both skidding. Driver and horse stopped, looked at each
> other, and the horse took off in the direction it came, as fast
> as before.
>
> * * *
>
> Today a pickup truck drove up Broadway carrying a
> huge black sleigh in the back.

Stranger than Fiction is one of the key elements in good
essay writing, and the person who goes out with his eyes open for
something unusual is likely to find it—again and again. Writing
that satisfies keeps coming up with little surprises. But beware the
fake surprise, like the observation of a Massachusetts girl that
"one minute it was clear and blue, when suddenly the sky was
growling and dark with rain clouds." That's not especially surprising in New England, where the weather can change minute
by minute. Though "growling" is a nice touch, the surprise and
drama of the moment that the writer wants to convey are false.
The most common form of false surprise withholds information

unnecessarily: "Mr. Pettifoggle was walking down Columbus Avenue minding his own business when It Happened." That's just cheating a reader. Far better and more honest a surprise to write, "When Mr. Pettifoggle was walking down Columbus Avenue minding his own business, a bread truck whipped around the corner and deposited a loaf of pumpernickel at his feet."

LETTER WRITING

Compiling gems of observation and conversation for your notebook is a good warm-up. So is writing letters, partly because letters teach you to write for readers. Letter writing is an art in itself, whose purpose is very similar to the college essay's: to show someone who you are, what you're thinking, and how things are with you. Sometimes you'll begin a letter, and quickly another idea will come to you. Put the letter aside—you can always go back to it—and follow the new thought. (That's not very gracious, I suppose, but you've got your future to think of. Your friend will understand.)

RAMBLING AND RANTING

Here's another good warm-up:

Rambling

In ten minutes, fill a notebook page with everything you're thinking. Keep your reader—friend, brother, teacher—in mind, and write fast, without stopping, and don't worry about shifting topics or ideas. Roam that inner landscape. If you get stuck, look around and write about what you see (sitting near a window is sometimes helpful—the outer landscape), or simply repeat your last line until something new comes to you. If it's good, show it to your reader. If it's disconnected, or boring, or bad, don't worry. This is batting practice. You're just trying to make contact, not hit home runs.

We went to Boston (family) to see the bar mitzvah of a friend of ours. It was pretty interesting—first one I've ever been to. No chopped liver sculptures or anything. I sort of missed the eighth grade rush at school, arriving a wee bit late. We saw the Renoir exhibit in Boston. Lots of lovely long-haired ladies and blue-eyed children. He's amazing with faces—he paints people I could stare at for hours. But when he sits a girl on a chair, it looks like she's floating a millionth of an inch above it. He just can't seem to get people to sit right in their armchairs. I've never seen so many people in a museum. In class today we talked about an essay I hadn't read. Actually, I read the wrong one. We were talking about hedgehogs and foxes and I read about Tolstoy and the Enlightenment.

It's rambling and fragmented, but there's an honest voice here and sharp details. It's alive. Any of the topics would be worth expanding later and could find their way into a college essay—the first bar mitzvah, reading the wrong essay, museums.

Rambling 2

Try pointing ten minutes of writing toward one topic. If detours appear in your path, follow them, but try to stay generally on course. Write as fast as you can and *don't stop*. Here's a senior remembering an eighth-grade teacher:

Mr. Newcombe carried a light tan leather briefcase with a slightly battered flap and he'd shuffle around in it until he got his papers organized, then he would snap shut the top and we'd see a pile of old yellow faded papers that looked as though they were from around the period that he was discussing. Then his wrist-breaking lectures began. It's strange the way Mr. Newcombe used and handled chalk. He always carried a bunch of colors to draw Greek battle plans with, and each one had a shiny chalk holder because he said he didn't want the chalk to dry out his fingers or make them purple or green. When Mr. Newcombe was missing a holder he would never switch them because it would waste too much time. Instead he held the bare chalk with the tips of his fingers, with his pinky raised in the air. It looked like he was waiting for a bird to perch on it.

Here are good details—"wrist-breaking lectures"—and surprising and funny comparisons. Naturally, it's rough. For exam
ple, "strange" is a vague word, "make" is weak, "chalk" is
overused, and "each one" could refer to battle plans or colors. The
whole entry has no real coherence, and a few sentences run on.
But it's still a lively notebook piece.

You can tell a story in your free writing:

> Buses were late this afternoon again. Our bus didn't show at
> 5:40. 6:00 still nothing. 6:30 Mr. Alexander comes out, tells
> us well, you see, the buses got stuck, another hour or two,
> etc. etc. Meanwhile it's Faculty-Trustee dinner night. So Gill
> and I saunter over and find Coach and Crawford. Mrs.
> Maresco brought us some stuffed mushrooms. Mr. Gucker
> said, "Hey, no problem, join the party! Here, have
> something to drink." My respect for him rose rapidly. 7:34
> the bus finally arrives. 7:53 around 180th Street, a guy starts
> running after us shouting, "Yo, yo, you're on fire, yo, you're
> *on fire!!*" Lance decides this a good enough reason to run
> around the bus screaming at the top of his fat little lungs.
> Bus driver stops, gets everyone off the bus, tries to see
> where the fire is. Decides he better call the company, but lo
> and behold, buses have no two-way radios. So he jumps on
> the bus and drives away, presumably to the nearest
> telephone, leaving forty of us standing in a rather
> conspicuous group on the corner. Gill and I say Bleep this,
> take a few 9th graders with us and bum a ride on the city
> bus. Got home at 8:45. Mom was throwing fits.

Remember, this is just the raw material. Think of your ramblings
as snapshots; if you write something good, you can show it to
your readers. If it's bad, shove it in a drawer. But even in dull
pieces, one or two lines will be vivid or memorable. Keep track
of them with checks in the margins or by bracketing or underlin-
ing, and soon a higher percentage of good sections will begin to
appear. You'll find yourself salvaging chunks of your ramblings
and notebook entries for the foundation of your college essay.

Free Association

This is more fun with a partner or a group. You both pick the
same ordinary object—a dish, a book, a saw, an egg—and really

look at it and think about it. Write the word at the top of a page. Then, in one minute, make a list of words and phrases the object brings to mind. Make the list as long as you can in one minute; don't leave anything out. Exchange lists. Did you have any of the same associations? Although you're bound to have some overlap, you'll also have wild differences. Each of us has a personal vocabulary of associations with even the most common things in our lives—a vocabulary that a writer frequently returns to for material.

Take one association or a series of them that seem connected, and write fast for fifteen minutes about the object. You might want to praise it, or attack it, or defend it from people who don't like it, or bring up something new about it that no one ever notices, or tell a story about it. Remember to write for your partner's entertainment.

That's a simple way to collect material to build an essay on—exploring what you already know. Try it with something that means a lot to you, like a bicycle or a favorite hat. You might remember how you got the hat, other hats you've had, why you like hats in general, why you like this hat in particular, what the point is of wearing a hat at all.

Grousing

Read John Updike's "Beer Can" on page 126. In fifteen minutes, write about something that has changed for the worse during your life. Describe the way it used to be and compare it to the present. If you want, begin with "Consider the———." In a different piece, write about something that has changed for the better.

Boring for Fun

Write fast for ten minutes about the dullest thing you do in the course of a day. Be as detailed as possible. A piece about boredom must be especially lively—don't try to show boredom by creating it. Make a reader feel, for instance, the exquisite torture of sitting through Mr. Snoozleman's lectures on the Punic Wars.

Ranting

Write from anger for ten minutes. Work on one topic or jump around—just keep writing and stay angry.

Your college essay may be buried somewhere in one of these suggestions, waiting to be unearthed. Time to get shoveling.

A FEW WORDS ON WRITER'S BLOCK

This mythic monster, which supposedly devours so much great work before it gets started, is not so ferocious as it is painted. I was tempted to say it doesn't exist at all, but then, in trying to show exactly how it doesn't exist, I got all tangled up and couldn't write a word.

But I'm still a writer's block agnostic; I doubt the existence of the old monster, which was always portrayed as kin to stage fright. I want to change the terms of the discussion. To begin to work, a writer needs to feel the freedom to write badly. Writer's block is nothing more than the loss of this freedom. Somehow, it vanishes. What happens is this: first you start picking over whether to use "but" or "however," when you should be chasing your thoughts across the landscape of your mind; then, very soon—too soon—after you've begun, instead of plunging forward you are crossing out everything you've written that day. Suddenly every sentence you think of is so full of obvious faults that you can't bear even to write one down. The blank page stares at you stupidly, infuriatingly, a reproachful mirror of your own blank mind.

But good writing not only does spring from bad, it must. *Keep going forward.* You can always cross things out later. "I have rewritten—often several times—every word I have ever published," said Vladimir Nabokov, the great novelist. "My pencils outlast their erasures." Writers know they write badly at first. But because we rarely see what's in their wastebaskets, we sometimes forget how badly. Ernest Hemingway said he rewrote the end of *A Farewell to Arms* thirty-nine times.

I'll say it again: first write, no matter how badly; rewrite and edit later. If you feel stuck, use the Rambling device of repeating your last sentence. If that doesn't work, take a ten-minute break: eat an apple, take a shower, play pinball, do squat thrusts. Then come back to it.

Don't expect your first draft to be a masterpiece. In the next chapters you'll see how writing comes alive gradually in the rewriting.

6 Coming Alive

Pump life into your essays with a few techniques borrowed from professionals.

TELL A STORY

All the world is not a stage; it's an audience, and it dearly loves a story. Professional writers know this, and use stories and pieces of stories, or *anecdotes*, to bring their work to life. An incident, a bit of conversation, a few vivid characters (real though they are) can be the difference between a lifeless piece and one that sings. Certainly a fragment of dialogue in a college essay—how rare it is!—is like catnip to an admissions officer.

So tell a story in your essay—tell three.

WHOLE SOLE

I had never even seen a whole sole before, and there were bones where bones just did not seem to belong. The Charbonneaus (that's what I'll call them) were obviously treating my first night with them as a special occasion—the tablecloth showed fresh creases, there was too much silverware, and the candles that had just been lit were tall and smooth. The only problem was that I really didn't like fish, and the knowledge of how to filet them was not a standard part of the education of a New

Jersey girl. But Monsieur and Madame smiled
indulgently at me, he with yellow teeth and she with a
gold one; I couldn't tell if they meant it or were only
making up for Catherine, their daughter, who looked my
way as if she might spit.

The candlelight was nice but I wished they had
turned the lights on, because romantic semi-darkness and
first-time fish fileting were not a good mix. All three of
them effortlessly lifted the flesh in one piece off the bone,
but I couldn't figure out where to put my fork. And then
I realized that I was supposed to use my knife. After I'd
broken its back and embedded tiny pieces of bone into
the flesh—mine and the fish's—I saw I was losing the
battle. So did Catherine, who finally had something to
smile about—entertainment tonight, guest starring the
American and a badly mauled fish.

Unfortunately I wasn't feeling very funny. I was
trying too hard not to seem like another provincial
American. Disregarding my first impulse—to deposit my
mouthful into the napkin—and my second—to cry—I
followed my third instinct and went to the bathroom,
trying to make as little fuss as possible.

The night before I left for the Experiment in
International Living, my parents had taken me to see
E.T. As I cried in the backseat on the way home they
were quick to say "Don't worry, Niki. If it's really bad
you can come home." It was nice of them to say it, but
none of us believed it for a minute. When I was in third
grade the same two people had made me stick it out at
Camp Waziyatah (which, I still remind my parents with
satisfaction, folded the next year). I guess some of my
tears were for Elliot, the boy in the movie, who had to
manage alone in the end. But at least he got to stay home.

Growing up in Tenafly, New Jersey, means that
Harold the mailman calls my mother by her first name
and all of Bob's Taxi drivers know who lives at 124
Churchill Road; and yes, the sole all comes boneless
from the market. Which is to say Tenafly is sheltered,
and there isn't much room for developing either
independence or filetmanship.

A feeling of security is what you do develop in

Tenafly and that feeling comes from living in the
comfort of a stable cocoon of familiarity. I didn't feel
secure in front of Catherine, or even in front of
something as harmless as a fish. In fact I felt like an
extra-terrestrial and I wanted to go home. But gradually,
picking bones out of my teeth in the bathroom, I looked
at the big picture. I realized I was not here to learn to
debone a fish; Julia Child could have taught me that in
my Tenafly living room. Of course, I wasn't sure what I
was here to do, if anything, but I knew this was part of
it.

When I emerged, I saw my dinner lying as I had
left it, unromantically half-clawed in the candlelight, and
for a moment my resolution shook like a weak muscle; I
had a quick idea of running out the door and back to the
train and the plane and New Jersey. M. Charbonneau
seemed a little puzzled but not especially interested in
whatever dilemma I was having. But his wife looked up
sympathetically as I neared the table. "Ça va?" she said.

Out of the corner of my eye, I saw Catherine smirk
again.

I sat down. I put a piece of sole on my fork. "Ça
va," I said. "Passez du vin, s'il vous plait."

The I's are frequent, and it's a Trip essay, but this writer gets
away with it because she tells a vivid story. She makes us feel the
strange new atmosphere by her choice of small details—the parents' teeth, the fish, Catherine's expression. But more than that,
the story is clearly going somewhere—not to a moral, but to a
point. She doesn't have to tell us "I conquered a difficult experience," because she shows it. She gives us an eye on the experience
and spares us the Trumpets of Triumph, or the Marvelous Me
Moral. She just tells what happened.

Writing this kind of story is largely a matter of choosing the
right incidents, and then letting them speak for themselves. The
temptation is always to finish with the sell job, the Trip trap:

"That summer taught me more than ever the importance of
learning to get along with many different kinds of people and the
necessity of self-reliance. I believe these qualities will be essential
in college."

Resist such conclusions at all costs. Events are complicated, and any attempt to squeeze Trumpets of Triumph out of them violates the reader's trust that you must work so hard to build.

The uses of anecdote are many:

a. the introduction and takeoff point for the whole essay.

b. a final note, a story that sums up or crystallizes what you have been saying and leaves a reader with the tone of the whole.

c. a detail in the body of the essay. Anecdotes used this way should not require a big windup. Be economical—save words, save readers.

d. a big story that runs throughout the the essay and shapes the whole. The filetmanship writer sandwiches her thoughts between the pieces of one story—the way movies use flashback technique: she's here in France, then she's back in America at a movie, then she's back again in France.

In a short piece like a college essay, anecdotes are a quick and vivid way to entertain and inform. Be careful about squeezing a story to fit a Marvelous Me Moral, and put a mute on Trumpets of Triumph. End with dialogue, like the essay above, or with an action reported.

ENTERTAINMENT QUOTIENT

After you have written short sketches like the ones in chapter five and are thinking of rewriting them or expanding them into full-scale college essays, look at them with a critical eye for their Entertainment Quotient:

1. Sense detail. Write to help admissions officers see what you saw, hear what you heard, taste what you tasted. Rather than tell what you learned from photography, show what it looks and feels and even sounds like in a darkroom as your picture emerges—the smell of the chemicals, the red bulb glowing in the darkness. Rather than describe how disciplined you have become as a result of your music lessons, talk about your violin itself, the texture and feel of it, the smell of the rosin and the wood—no one ever thinks of the sense of smell in connection with a violin—details that put a reader through your practice routine with you. Sight, sound, smell, touch, taste. In other words, show what you know.

2. Metaphor. Writers continually see one thing in terms of something else; the result is metaphor, the language of comparison. Sometimes the sheer wit and power of metaphors can carry a piece of writing and make it entertaining and fresh, and learning to think metaphorically is perhaps the most "fun" part of writing. You need to have command of the two common ways of making comparisons. One simply uses "like" or "as": *The leaves are like hands.* The other speaks directly: *The leaves are hands;* or, more subtly, *The leaves beckoned in the wind.* (The metaphor is contained in the verb; leaves don't usually beckon—but they might if they're like hands.) Metaphors are all around you, but through time and use some of them have lost their ability to startle: leg of a chair, face of a clock, eye of a needle. Still others are on their way to the metaphor graveyard but are not quite buried yet. Using them is not the sign of dead metaphor but of a dead mind: white as snow, big as a mountain, high as a kite, smooth as glass. There are thousands of others. To be an entertaining writer you must hammer your own metaphor out of materials you know and understand. A good rule of thumb, suggested by George Orwell, author of *1984,* is never to use a comparison you have heard before.

3. Verbs and Nouns. Nouns are the bones of writing; verbs are the muscles. Entertaining writing gets its structure and strength from them. Don't load up on adjectives—a *"wondrous* evening," a *"multifaceted* personality"—hoping to sound more "creative" or intelligent. An essay flabby with adjectives only weighs a reader down. Before you can write beautifully you must write well. Try the following:

Without adjectives ("the," "an," and "a" are OK), write a short paragraph or two describing something—a restaurant, a teacher, a pen, a bird, your favorite room in the house—so that it sounds appealing. Then—again without adjectives—make the same subject unappealing. It will seem awkward at first; remember, nothing comes out whole, and it will take a few drafts to trim and tighten the paragraph. But you'll increase your control over words and style. Here's an example:

[1]

There's nothing on the planet like chocolate. Vanilla may be the province of the purist and the test of the connoisseur, but in the kingdom of sweets, darkness rules. Among the garden of edibles, chocolate earns the status of sin—a compliment, like knowledge itself in the Garden of Eden. A silk among desserts, its flavor is like a mixture of malt and nectar and cream.

[2]

People who like chocolate must be in league with dentists, the pokers and pullers who have inherited the reins of torture from the Inquisition. Is chocolate worth the pain? I don't think so. It appeals to children who, when the temperature inches up and softens fudge, like to fingerpaint Uncle Nathan's belly with it. It doesn't look like dessert then; it looks more like something the dog deposits. To adults I've seen scrambling for the Toblerone, it's like a drug. Not for nothing is the cacao, from which it is pounded, related to cocaine.

These examples are admittedly freaks. In your final essays you needn't carry adjective-bashing to this extreme, but it's fun to noodle with; this is a true literary pushup that will make your writing stronger.

When you learn to rely on verbs and nouns, they keep you thinking metaphorically, as you can see from the examples. Increasing your store of verbs and nouns opens up that world of comparison. For example, the verb "fasten" might be *pin, stitch, chain, paste, moor, clasp, clamp, suture,* or *belay* (from mountain climbing), depending on the comparison you wanted to suggest. One of my classes found 148 synonyms for the word "walk"—a good many more than are found in any thesaurus. Make a list of your own with a friend or two. Think metaphorically: How does a horse on parade walk? How does a thief walk? A snake? Try the same thing with the word "say."

METAPHOR MADNESS

Children are natural metaphorists. On a walk in the woods in late fall, the four-year-old son of a friend looked up (from his vantage atop his father's shoulders) at all the branches around him losing their leaves and said, "The trees have their pants down."

Kids are always reporting what they see in fresh language; they haven't learned how to be dull. We grow up into dullness, just the way we lose the imaginary friends that we sometimes had as kids. But kids don't know what they're saying and can't build on it; with them, metaphor is simple habit, part of the way they think. In one sense, learning to write is learning to recover the freshness and imagination of kid talk and harnessing it to grown-up consistency.

You can help redevelop the metaphorical habit by doing what kids (and writers) do—playing games. I call one Fruits and Vegetables, a good one for long car or train rides with friends or family. To start, the one who's "it" thinks of a person you all know, like a figure from history, a teacher, or a neighbor, and says only "a teacher" or "historical female." The others must try to guess who it is by asking metaphorical questions: "What kind of vegetable would he be?" (It's more fun as a game than as an interview.) You must respond with an answer that in your mind reflects the essence of the person, not just a superficial characteristic. For example, don't answer "red pepper" simply because the subject has red hair. Better to answer pepper if the subject has a spicy and colorful personality. Questioners should really stretch—which type of bird would he be, which highway in America, which breakfast food, which household appliance. Each guesser is allowed only one guess before he is out, but there is no limit to the number of questions.

Here's another good metaphor game for those long rides. I call it Raymond Chandler, in honor of the mystery writer known for his similes. You may need pencil and paper at first, but soon you'll be able to play it in your head. Begin with two columns of nouns, one concrete, the other abstract. For example:

hammer	honesty
piano	love
light bulb	trust
birdseed	disappointment
rowboat	tension

Your friend picks one word from column A, one from B, and both of you make a sentence that shows why they're alike: Love is like a light bulb: you can turn it off and on. Or, Love is like a rowboat: it takes hard work to keep it moving forward. Or, Love is like a piano: you have to practice to be good. Writers are constantly indulging this playfulness with ideas and words, and the metaphors, forced as they are, sometimes uncover strange truths you never saw before.

Play the same game with things you care about:

soccer
books
college
teachers
sleep

Match them with nouns at random: shirt, glass, key, tiger, dinner.

Robert Frost, the poet, played this game. "Poets," he said, "are like baseball pitchers. Both have their moments. The intervals are the tough things." So did E. B. White: "A writer is like a bean plant—he has his little day, and then gets stringy."

Don't worry about stretching it to ridiculous limits—that's how you get better and better at seeing connections and playing with ideas.

"Aw, c'mon, Mr. Bauld, that's b.s.," my students sometimes complained when we played these games. "Everything can't be like everything else." I couldn't agree more; it is b.s. And inferior b.s. is a very shoddy product. But I want to defend b.s., so often hooted at by seniors, because when b.s. reaches a certain (very high) level, it is called thinking, and when it finds a voice, it is called literature. The college essay demands a good dose of medium-high-level b.s., and I urge you to cultivate a superior strain of it as soon as you can and with as much care as you can muster.

7 Sweetheart, Get Me Rewrite!

In old movies, the grizzled reporter at the scene of the crime—the leg man—races to a pay phone and shoves in his nickel. "Sweetheart," he rasps when the gum-popping receptionist answers in the newspaper office, "get me rewrite!" Then he barks a few garbled facts to a team of rewrite specialists who turn out something snappy and readable. *Time* magazine still works essentially this way. Wouldn't it be great to shout a few thoughts into a telephone and a day later have a college essay come back? But it's unlikely that you have a staff of people wearing sleeve guards and green eyeshades poised in your living room waiting to punch up your copy. Sweetheart, you *are* rewrite.

Writers revise in different ways. I have a friend, a novelist, who rewrites his entire draft three times from beginning to end, by hand. He says that's a good way to run it whole through his mind. He is also a stickler for working with heavy paper and fine fountain pens. Other writers, having finished a draft, go to work with scissors, tape, and felt-tip marker, moving paragraphs around, crossing out, adding phrases and sentences, jotting notes in the margins. Some write and revise completely on a word processor. Only by writing and rewriting often will you find the method of revision that works best for you.

Whatever your method, you know it's revision time when you've written a few pages and your draft begins to dull, like a knife in constant use. You're near the end, but suddenly you can't cut through the jungle of your thoughts, and you need to stop. It's important to keep writing fast until you've pushed a topic as far as it will go. But when you revise, things slow down a bit—not as slow as in the final editing, but a clear change in tempo from your draft. At the rewrite stage, good writers keep an essay alive by pausing to ask the right questions of themselves.

WHERE AM I?

You can teach yourself to be your own rewrite department. One way to find out where you are is to identify good lines. Always work initially from what's good. Also try writing down on a separate sheet the most important nouns and verbs in your draft. Reread all the metaphors. What do they suggest? These are just tricks to help you be aware of the landmarks you've left scattered around, in case you don't know where to go. Often, simply reading your draft carefully will be enough to plot the course ahead.

Can you find a main idea, reducible to a sentence or two, that can serve as your compass? Rereading his first draft, the writer in chapter four who lamented the passing of the sixties might have summed up his idea this way: "Let's not bury the sixties yet—at least not while I'm around."

You may find that a detour you took makes a better essay. Follow it. Or you may want to get back on your original course. Once you glimpse an idea in the distance again, think about rearranging your draft to plot the best way to get there. Sometimes that means a straight line, sometimes the scenic route. It helps to imagine that the path of your idea, like a forest trail seen from an airplane, creates (in your mind and a reader's) a *shape*.

WHAT SHAPE AM I IN?

All essays have shape, or form—not on the page, where they look alike, but in the mind, where they differ sharply. A point-by-point logical argument may climb down to its conclusion like steps; a humorous essay may sprout crazy petals from a center. An anecdotal piece may swerve briefly away from its main subject in an S-curve and finally point, as the tail of an S does, back to the beginning. Talking about shape this way is metaphorical, not literal, but readers sense the pattern (whether or not they realize it), and it puts them on firm footing.

Shape often comes *after* the first draft. You may have only a vague notion of shape—or none at all—as you begin, but it will gradually emerge from the writing, like a figure from a sculptor's block. You may find that what you have to say is shaped by the flow of one memory or experience, like the student essay on the stepmother in chapter eleven; or several smaller anecdotes may give it form, as in David Owen's "Pfft," in chapter twelve. Sometimes the shape begins to grow out of your revisions of the beginning and the end.

THE BEGINNING: HOW (AND WHEN)

Earlier I urged you to "start anywhere" when you begin to write a draft. Still true. But once you've written a couple of pages you need to think about what newspapers call a *lead,* which rhymes with seed, which is the function of your first sentence—to plant early in a reader's mind something that will bear fruit later. The worst thing a lead can be is *leaden,* which rhymes with deaden, which describes what a careless or dull lead does to readers and to your application. If your writing has only one chance to sparkle, it should sparkle at the beginning.

The irony about a good lead is that it is very often written *last.* That's right. It's frequently a product of revision. That's partly because (I repeat) writers don't usually know what they're going to say until they say it. Leads come last also because they're tough to do and they matter so much. Even the best writers stumble forward with a kind of prayer: Maybe one will come to me. And when they work at it enough, one usually does.

Some experienced writers do keep their eyes open for a lead as they write the draft. This is tricky. Working under frequent deadlines, a newspaper writer tries to find shortcuts, and working from a good lead gives the draft an immediate focus and often does away with the need for a lot of revision. But that's in the hands of those who do it for a living, every day. You can try it too, with this warning: The minute you slow down and start groping instead of writing fast, forget about the lead and push ahead.

Now and then, when you're really cooking, you will whip up a good lead right at the outset. If it comes, fine; if it doesn't, don't worry about it. Say to yourself, I'll write a lead if it's the last thing I do. It may be.

What is a good lead? For writers, a line or two that gives a shaping edge, an "angle," to an essay; for readers, something that nudges them into the rest of the piece. That's really all—something to stir up a reasonable amount of curiosity. Here's the first line of George Orwell's essay on England during World War II: "As I write, highly civilised human beings are flying overhead, trying to kill me." Only the subverbal would not read on. A *great* lead is something else—a memorable sentence in itself and the distilled essence of the essay. E. B. White began "Death of a Pig," perhaps the only good Pet Death essay ever written, with this: "I spent several days and nights in mid-September with an ailing pig and I feel driven to account for this stretch of time, more particularly since the pig died at last, and I lived, and things might easily have gone the other way round and none left to do the accounting." There's a seed lead for you—it contains the wry humor of the rest of the piece, a summation of the narrative, and a glimpse of the main idea: that the reminders of our own deaths are tragic and comic both.

A bad lead is all windup and no pitch: "In the following essay I hope to show . . ." Just *do* it, don't announce it. Or a false question: "Have you ever thought about bee pollen?" You know perfectly well your readers haven't thought about bee pollen. The false question rings hollow.

Look at the leads in chapters eleven and twelve. H. L. Mencken's use of one word, "infest," is startling enough to carry us into the story of his first memory. You may disagree with the suggestion contained in that word—that humans are pests in the universe's kitchen—but you'll read on.

Here are a few leads you might play with:

The Anecdote

Probably the most common beginning for an essay. As you saw in chapter six, a story or a snippet of dialogue is an extremely effective lead—as long as it bears on your topic. E. B. White's "Age of Dust" (see p. 126) opens with a seemingly innocent chord that later echoes in a different key. One girl began an essay about her father, "Every Sunday I wake up to a 1940s Prell Shampoo jingle sung in falsetto by a short, wiry, balding intellectual. My dad is a nut." Watch for anecdotal leads in newspaper features and magazine stories, and pay attention to how they work.

The Why? Lead

When the reader asks Why? In response to your lead, you're in business. "I try to live reasonably in the modern world, but it gets harder and harder." Why? In another of his essays, George Orwell begins, "In Moulmein, in Lower Burma, I was hated by large numbers of people—the only time in my life that I have been important enough for this to happen to me." Why?

The Shocker

For instance, "I do some of my best thinking in the bathroom" (p. 119). Nobody could pass up the rest of that essay. It's good to startle readers now and then. "I grew up a killer," might begin a light story of becoming a vegetarian.

But the Shocker is not simply any wild or fanciful statement; abused, it's just another *National Enquirer* headline. A good one steers a reader to the main idea of the essay. Use it like the loaded weapon it is, with care.

The Curmudgeon

A curmudgeon is a contrary person; the Curmudgeon lead is ornery, often a paradox. "*Moby Dick* may be a great book, but it is not a good book." You can skewer an immense number of conventional ideas if you're good at the Curmudgeon lead. Here's one by G. K. Chesterton (from around 1907): "I have no sympathy with international aggression when it is taken seriously, but I have a certain dark and wild sympathy with it when it is quite absurd." It doesn't have to be a paradox, though, as this lead from H. L. Mencken (curmudgeon of all curmudgeons) shows: "No man ever quite believes in any other man."

The Split

You can divide people or things into a few simple types. "There are those who have faith in man-made things and those who do not," wrote Ellen Goodman (p. 131). Ada Louise Huxtable began an article called "Modern-Life Battle: Conquering Clutter," with this: "There are two kinds of people in the world—those who have a horror of a vacuum and those with a horror of the things that fill it." Both writers may have been thinking of Charles Lamb's lead (almost 160 years ago): "The human species, according to the best theory I can form of it, is composed of two distinct races, the men who borrow, and the men who lend." It's a good device for a light essay. But always stay close to your own experience. The whole point of beginning this way is that you, too, fall into one of the categories.

The Raymond Chandler

Simply use a comparison like one of those from the game in chapter six. "The allurement that women hold out to men," begins a Mencken essay, "is precisely the allurement that Cape Hatteras holds out to sailors: they are enormously dangerous and hence enormously fascinating."

The Confession

David Owen's first sentence (p. 133), for example. The Confession lead is not *really* confessional—the aim isn't to reveal intimate details from a sense of guilt. You're trying to entertain, remember.

"I do some of my best thinking in the bathroom" is a Confession and a Shocker both. What makes the Confession lead effective is the honesty of the observation. By opening up a subject that you know other people—in Owen's case, people his age or older—recognize but don't talk about, you become the reader's confidant.

Stating the Obvious

I mean the obvious that is hidden, because it is right under our noses. In the lead to "Heavier than Air" (p. 124), White highlights the *weight* of a plane, something so obvious we never think about it. The essay is structured around the simple idea that a plane is *big*. The planes in George Orwell's lead are different from White's, though Orwell states the obvious in an equally startling way—of *course* the people flying a plane are highly civilized; *naturally* they are trying to kill him—there's a war on. But the line is striking, and makes us realize something we knew-but-didn't-know. A good Stating the Obvious lead might be something as simple as "San Francisco is a long way from New York." Well, now that you mention it, of course it is. Why do you bring it up?

Refer to this list—sketchy as it is—during revision, or make up variations of your own. I'll refer to it, too, when I get around to writing the introduction to this book. Maybe something will come to me.

ENDINGS

Let's look at the other pole. Once you hook readers, you've got to make sure to land them. Here's how you *don't* finish a piece: "in conclusion," "in summation," "finally," "I would like to close by saying," or any of the other staples from the Stylebook of the Dull.

The best endings remember where they came from, but they don't insult readers by calling attention to themselves or repeating what's already been said. Beginnings and endings *speak* to each other. "I do some of my best thinking in the bathroom" ends "Maybe they'd think of something." Even the sounds are alike: some thinking, think of something. Another of the Exhibits in chapter eleven (p. 101): "Except for my struggle with jacks—I could never get past sixies while Leslie Ackerman whizzed through tenzies and back to onezies all in one turn—this application is the greatest challenge I've faced." The end: "The whole thing makes sevenzies look easy."

The pros know the same secret. "This seems to be an era of gratuitous inventions and negative improvements," is Updike's lead on page 126, and his ending speaks to it: "What we need is Progress with an escape hatch."

Because of the close relationship between the beginning and the end, you may find yourself working on both of them simultaneously; in my magazine writing I have often discovered a good lead buried in what I originally thought was the ending.

Another way to end effectively is with an anecdote, as David Owen does (p. 134) in his piece about growing older. The quoted sound from his father—not even a word!—is surprising and memorable because it sums up so succinctly everything Owen himself has been feeling about growing older. Owen is here using a favorite device of reporters—letting someone else say what's also on the writer's mind.

I don't know for sure, but I'm guessing that Owen started with the quotation from his father—it goes back further in time than anything else he talks about—and wrote the rest of the piece "into" it. You can work the same way. Write your last sentence first—a strong line or two of dialogue—and then write the essay it completes.

Ending with a good quotation often gives a feeling of finality. The filet-frightened New Jersey girl in chapter six quotes herself and leaves us to judge from that how she handled her problem. In both her essay and David Owen's, we say the end-feeling works because the *rhythm* is good. Rhythm in writing refers to the length of sentences, which, in any good piece, should vary. Almost any rhythm, handled well, can work for the ending, but there are certain patterns that writers continually call on, just as there are final cadences and chords in a song or a symphony that let you know the music is ending. Many writers find the sound of finality in short sentences. Owen, Russell Baker (p. 131), Ellen Goodman (p. 132), and a few of the best student pieces in chapter eleven end with short, vigorous sentences. Especially effective endings often set up the last line with a long, slow sentence full of commas and twists of thought, followed by one or two short, brisk lines to close. Try it. (See?)

One warning about finishing with an anecdote or quotation. Make sure it bears closely on your main point. There are few things more confusing than an irrelevant story. If David Owen had ended his piece this way, it would have fallen flat:

> When my daughter and I were walking in the park recently, she bent to pick a yellow flower by the side of the path. "Look," she said, clutching the daisy and holding it out to me. "It's the sun."

There's nothing wrong with this story; it just doesn't complete the thought he's been developing.

In a college essay, the end is not quite as important as the beginning, but make sure your ending remembers where it came from and sounds final.

Hearing Your Own Voice: Revising Style

Your writing voice—the sound of your sentences—is your "style." It's a combination of your word choice, tone, and even your thought. But many individual styles fall into a few big divisions. Compare:

A. Please elaborate upon the circumstances surrounding the collision.

B. Describe the accident.

C. How'd you crash the car?

D. What went down with your wheels?

Four different ways of saying the same thing—four different voices. All can be the same serious, dispassionate tone, but the style is different.

A is formal—tuxedo talk. Scholars, lawyers, and people seeking to maintain a professional distance from their audience use it.

B is informal—a sweater, comfortable shoes. The voice is direct and unadorned.

C is colloquial—T-shirt and sneakers, the breeziness of everyday conversation.

D is slang—leather jackets, street talk.

We slip in and out of these styles as we talk, and in your first draft you'll probably find pieces of different styles. Good. In your first draft you are just getting the words out and should write in the voice that feels most comfortable. In revising, you must decide whether each shift in style is effective.

Work toward the informal. It is the most flexible voice, one that can be serious or light. On top of that bass line, you can play variations—just as you do with rhythm. Professional writers mix them skillfully, sometimes in a single sentence:

> This seems to be an era of gratuitous inventions and negative improvements. Consider the beer can.

The first line is strictly tuxedo, the second a plain pullover.

> Even by standards of that time it was a primitive place. There was no electricity. Roads were unpaved. In our house there was no plumbing. The routing of summer days was shaped by these deficiencies.

Four sweaters followed by a little hint of tails and top hat.

Dialogue usually wears T-shirt or leather jacket; few people speak with the directness of an informal style or the elevated sound of the formal.

> Rising dust along the road from the mountains signaled an approaching event. A car was coming. "Car's coming," someone would say.

Baker puts them back to back. "A car was coming. 'Car's coming.'"

When you reread your draft, be alert for shifts in your style—are these changes of dress effective, or should you be returning to your informal wardrobe? Although in your essays you should stay close to the informal, good writing moves back and forth easily among the different styles. In general steer clear of tuxedo talk—to write well in a formal style takes years. On the other hand, too much slang in an essay grates like too many car horns in traffic. You're looking for balance. One object of revision is to decide when you should go casual and when you should dress up, and to wear it all convincingly.

8 Tinkering

It's not always easy to say where rewriting (the Big Stuff) leaves off and editing (the Small Stuff) begins. For instance, I talk about style as Big Stuff and tone as Small, but the distinction, I confess, is almost arbitrary. As you'll see in chapter nine, an essay *evolves*, and the stages often blur. You probably won't be able to resist some tinkering when you rewrite. Like an auto mechanic, you'll notice a few small parts out of whack and start pulling here, twisting there, jiggling this connection, tightening that one, to make your prose engine run better, while a big problem in the exhaust system still waits. There's nothing wrong with that. We'd all like to be more organized, but we aren't. That goes double for writers.

Still, if you're going to be a good mechanic and not just another slob banging away with a wrench, it helps to have some idea what you're doing. There is value in remembering the separation of draft, rewrite, and edit. It can keep you from fussing with details when you should be thinking about what you're trying to say. Imagine the stages as different speeds in that vehicle you're fixing: Draft is overdrive, whipping along so fast the view is a blur—you're just trying to hold on around the corners; rewrite is travel gear, steady but slower, good for seeing the whole panorama; and editing is a stop-and-go crawl that gives you every bit of scenery in detail for as long as you want.

A good college essay—or any piece of writing—needs careful editing to develop. Just as you can learn to be your own rewrite department, you can be your own best editor.

TONE: HOW TO WIN FRIENDS AND INFLUENCE ADMISSIONS OFFICERS

Tone, in writing and speaking, is the same—your *mood.* Admissions officers read your essay to discover the "type of person" you are, and your mood is one very transparent clue. Learn to control the tone of your writing voice the way you control the tone of your speaking voice; you wouldn't want your boy- or girl-friend to think you were bitter or sarcastic when you felt friendly and forgiving. That's how misunderstandings start, and you can't kiss and make up with admissions officers.

Remember your audience. Would you boast at a party to someone you were attracted to—"Hi, I've really made myself a better person lately. I really know how to handle challenges"? Unlikely—unless you wanted to test how fast he or she could politely find someone else to talk to. Don't boast in your essay. Many students do, on the mistaken premise that they must sell themselves.

Don't whine. "I have some teachers who are mean, but others are all right." Don't plead. "I think First Choice is a great school and I've really wanted to go there for as long as I can remember." Pleaders are described by admissions officers as "sweaty." Controlling your tone means being sensitive to the effect of your words on a reader. Compare three possible lines you might use to explain poor performance in one class:

A. I can't stand physics.

B. Physics is a stupid science.

C. Physics is a mystery to me.

All may represent the truth as you see it, and you might say any one of them to a close friend who forgives you your little peeves. But which would you use with Mr. Quark, the physics teacher, sitting across from you? The tone of A is aggressive, and B insulting. At least C, which expresses an honest humility, gives you a chance of being heard without raising the teacher's hackles. Change the audience again. Which is best for talking to that hypothetical person I keep bringing up—someone you are attracted to but don't know well? (Specifically, you don't know whether he or she is a physics wiz. And you *really* want to get to know this person better.) A *could* work—but it would have to precede a pretty entertaining rap to be winning. B is out of the question—whiny and dumb. C in this case could express awe and wonder—your best bet to sound like an interesting person.

What kind of tone should you use in your college essay? Whatever suits you. Even stubborn can work, if you know you're stubborn and don't take yourself too seriously. A writer doesn't pick his tone from a menu—"I think I'll be bittersweet today, because I plan to be ironic tomorrow." The mood grows out of the subject and the writer's authentic feeling about it. But a writer learns to recognize through practice what sounds right, just as you have developed an instinct for the right way to talk to different friends. If you try to sound friendly and you don't feel that way, it always sounds fake—to you and, you can be sure, to your audience.

In "Beer Can" (p. 126), John Updike sounds weary from having achieved a ruffled, temporary truce with the modern world. Mencken, on the other hand, is gruff and outright crabby, even though he's only recording his first memory. Ellen Goodman is resigned to her phobias. Fran Lebowitz mocks the straight, helpful tone of pop psychology. E. B. White's "Heavier than Air" is a gentle scolding.

But there is no fail-safe tone that will prevent you from bombing. I could say that admissions officers always like a tone that is Nice-and-Friendly, or Respectful, or Enthusiastic. It would make sense, but it wouldn't be entirely accurate. *Trying* to sound Nice or Respectful or Enthusiastic, like trying to be funny or clever, doesn't work. For one thing, Nice and Respectful turn easily into Boring and Sweaty, and Enthusiastic into Fluffy. Admissions officers will like who you are if you give them—and yourself—a chance. Remember the natural voice. You can only be who you are and have the moods you have. Concentrate on using your moods to produce something entertaining and revealing.

Read your draft aloud—in what tone of voice would you say your lines? What do your chosen readers have to say about it? The good thing about writing is that if it sounds whiny or brittle or just plain fake, you can change it. Just like that.

DICTION

Diction is word choice, one source of tone. A diction*ary*, one source of words, nourishes a writer. A thesaurus, on the other hand—a list or a book of synonyms without definitions—is a cauldron of chemical flavorings. Words extracted from the thesaurus (and not organically grown in your head) may sound good. But artificial flavorings can also cause disease, and people who know the anatomy of prose can easily see the cancerous lumps forming in your writing. Too many college essays are choked with "myriad"s, "plethora"s, and other test-tube words:

> A student's scholastic experience encompasses a multitude of endeavors.

Yecch. It's not entirely your fault—this elephantiasis of the word infects more than college essays. Even baseball players (and announcers), usually so vivid, have caught it: a pitcher no longer has "speed" or "smoke" on his fastball, he now has "good velocity." This is plain bad, an attempt by insecure people to sound educated. Velocity certainly doesn't sound any faster than speed—we don't talk about something moving at "the velocity of light," which is a good deal quicker than even Dwight Gooden's best. (In physics, technically, velocity and speed aren't even interchangeable, though baseball people don't know that.) Perhaps because players today earn salaries ten times as high as in 1937, they think they deserve more expensive words to describe their pitches. But inflated language doesn't make the fastballs any faster; it just makes the speaker sound pretentious and dumb. Get good value from your words.

By all means *learn more words*—by reading more, and by listening to people who speak clearly and vividly. That's the only way you'll understand how to use them. (Nobody—no *writer*—learns words from vocabulary lists.) Sometimes it means training your ear to distinguish the lively from the flat when both come from the same source. Ballplayers today, for instance, also say a fast pitcher "throws heat," or is "a flame thrower," two pointed and colorful metaphors.

Another way to build your cache of words is to learn the exact names of things you touch and see every day. For instance, here are some good words that name common parts of a house: cornice, dormer, gable, widow's walk, garret, wing, gutter, shutter, clapboard, eave. Though you probably see these architectural details every day, how many of them do you recognize by name? Knowing—and using—the names for the parts of a boat, of a church, of a flower, of a cow, of everything around you, helps your language come alive.

One warning: In your word researches, lean toward the plain and solid word where you have a choice between it and a more scientific-sounding one; of the two words for a dolphin's nose, for example, *beak* is more vigorous than *rostrum,* and the implied comparison with birds even catches something of a dolphin's playfulness.

Good writing knows the names of things, and good words are accurate and lively. I guarantee that if you are reading this book, you already know enough words to write a good essay.

But even among familiar words, not all are created equal. A few have come to mean so little—not only in college essays (though especially there) but also in memos, letters, speeches, and conversation—that they are almost meaningless. These you must un-learn:

interpersonal	commitment
interact	leadership (and "leadership
responsibility	role")
excellence	individual goals (in place of
integrity	*person*)
diversity	aspect
situation	factor
relationship	endeavor
bottom line	tendency
utilize	considerable
values	

There are many more, and I don't even have room for empty phrases like "at the present time" (which should be simply "now" or "today"). Many applicants use these puffs of smoke in a wrong-headed effort to appear intelligent and worthy of admission. But language like this is the hallmark of people who have nothing to say and usually know it. "I have come to admire and respect him," wrote one New York politician of another recently, "for his commitment to values we all cherish in American life." The words are like incense, filling the air with pretty-smelling smoke that drowns every whiff of the sharper, less pleasant odor of truth. Which values? How does he know we *all* "cherish" them? Who's we? Can someone be committed to values? What does that mean?

Some of the words on my list are bad because they are jargon, like *bottom line*. Some are pretentious, like *utilize* and *individual*. Some are so vague we never know what their purpose is in a sentence: *situation, aspect, commitment*. Like so many feathers, these words just take up space and insulate us from meaning. Others have been degraded by dishonesty and overuse: *integrity, excellence, responsibility,* words so often used to describe criminals, incompetence, and evasiveness that they make literate people laugh. They are almost always used to manipulate an audience, not communicate. Here are other smoke balls:

obviously	virtually
clearly	unquestionably
rather	particularly
somewhat	relatively
kind of, sort of	

Bad writers love to begin a paragraph with "Clearly . . ." But if it is clear, don't say so; just show it and stop stacking the deck against the reader. If it is not clear—which it usually isn't when "Clearly . . ." raises its ugly head—then saying so is dishonest. *Clearly, obviously, unquestionably* are loaded dice intended to cheat the reader.

I was kind of tired

Megan is rather opinionated.

That's a somewhat risky endeavor.

More cheating, here from cowardice rather than emptiness or deception. Don't waffle. If you have something to say, say it: I was tired. Megan is opinionated. That's risky.

Clearly, in the rush of your draft you will use many words that don't pull their weight. Obviously, you can revise out all sloppiness, all smoke screens, all cheating. Unquestionably, you will write a better essay if you do.

TRANSITIONS

Writing transitions is the art of getting from here to there and back in your thoughts without jolting the reader out of his seat. Think of your essay as a chain. Each link (idea, anecdote, description) is complete in itself and yet is also part of the one before and the one after. Many of the usual devices for connecting parts of an essay are useful and quick if not skillful: *but, instead, now, later, then.* But others are clanky: *nevertheless, therefore, moreover, in addition, thus, more important, secondly* (and *thirdly*), *finally,* and other formal, archaic-sounding words. They clank because, like chains in the attic, they carry the sound of deadness.

Sometimes you can't avoid the ordinary devices. Updike, the least clanky of writers, calls on them in making transitions in "Beer Can": although he shifts simply from present to past with the use of "was" in his third sentence, he brings back the present with "Now we are given, instead." Then "However" and "But" take us into the future. But because the shifts are quick, the words do not call attention to themselves, and we hardly notice the transitions at all. That's the goal.

In "Summer Beyond Wish" (p. 128), Russell Baker doesn't even try to make smooth transitions. He moves from scene to scene like a filmmaker, in sharp cuts. He can do this because he's arranged his images in gradually increasing importance and because he's followed the sequence of a day—morning images first, then afternoon happenings, and then evening.

Transitions connect or contrast time or thought. Sketch the big movements of your essay, the way an artist suggests with a few broad strokes the main shapes in his composition. Is the piece an If . . . but no . . . therefore essay? Or is it in two sections, Once . . . but now? Or a simple time sequence: This . . . then this . . . then this? There are as many formats as there are essays. Charting the main transitions in your draft can help you polish its shape.

TRIMMING THE FAT: AN ABSURDLY BRIEF GUIDE

Many college essays are bloated with sentences that could be tightened or completely eliminated. When you've got only five hundred words—and often fewer—to nourish readers, every one must count.

In other words, *simplify.* Here are ways to reduce the most unsightly sentence fat.

1. *Who, which, that,* and *what* often swell a sentence with blubber. Use them only when necessary.

FAT:
Uncle Nathan is someone who cares only about fly fishing.

TRIM:
Uncle Nathan cares only about fly fishing.

FAT:
Todd had a dog which he took on long walks.

TRIM:
Todd took his dog on long walks.

FAT:
What Betty hoped was that the president would admit a mistake.

TRIM:
Betty hoped the president would admit a mistake.

2. *There* and *it* are often unnecessary.

FAT:
There were geese swimming on the pond.

TRIM:
Geese swam on the pond.

FAT:
It is the love of fly fishing that keeps Uncle Nathan going.

TRIM:
Love of fly fishing keeps Uncle Nathan going.

FAT:
At the end of the play there was a groan from the audience.

TRIM:
At the end of the play the audience groaned.

3. Be alert for fatty uses of the word *thing*.

FAT:
The thing I'm interested in is science.

TRIM:
I'm interested in science.

4. Trimming *thing* in that example also allowed me to cut *is*. Lazy uses of *is, am, were, was, are,* and the other forms of the verb *to be,* can cause ugly sentence spread.

FAT:
Fifty years ago, it was natural for athletes to play before adoring crowds.

TRIM:
Fifty years ago, athletes expected to play before adoring crowds.

FAT:
In a telephone survey it was shown that there is little support for secret operations.

TRIM:
A telephone survey revealed little support for secret operations.

The verb *to be* is not always so expendable. But be careful with it. Check your drafts to make sure every use of *to be* pulls its own weight.

5. Cut *second helpings*. When you're trying to get your prose into shape, needless restatements overstuff a sentence.

FAT:
My brother is an honest person. That's a quality I respect in him.

TRIM:
I respect my brother's honesty.

We know honesty is a quality and your brother is a person.

Try cutting out the second helpings in this paragraph:

> A piano is a temperamental thing. The unpredictable nature
> of this instrument is apparent to anyone who has an old
> one, as we do. My mom's big upright has good days, when it
> sounds like a concert grand. It also has bad days, when the
> keys become stiff or sticky as a result of slight changes in
> humidity, and it never quite acts the same under different
> conditions. It's often as stubborn as a mule. When the
> temperature is colder, the tone has a harder character than
> when it is warm. At these times it makes sounds more like
> something being tortured.

Double helpings: We know a piano is a thing. "The unpredicta-
ble nature of this instrument" treads the same ground as the
first sentence. "It never quite acts the same under different conditions" is completely unnecessary. A rewrite might look like
this:

> An old piano is as temperamental as a mule. On good days
> my mom's big upright sounds like a concert grand. But
> when the humidity changes quickly, the keys stiffen and
> stick and the tone hardens, and it whines and groans as if
> tortured.

6. *Replace vague verbs.* Remember, verbs are the muscles of
writing. *Become, get, do, make,* and *have* are weak muscles; they
don't generate motion or action. Reread the two paragraphs
above.

WEAK:
the keys become stiff or sticky

STRONG:
the keys stiffen and stick

WEAK:
the tone has a harder character

STRONG:
the tone hardens

WEAK:
it makes sounds more like something being tortured.

STRONG:
it whines and groans as if tortured.

7. *Replace passive verbs.* Use the active voice. The passive voice fattens on lazy uses of *to be:*

PASSIVE:
Gooden's next pitch was lined by Boggs into left.

ACTIVE:
Boggs lined Gooden's next pitch into left.

PASSIVE:
This bread was baked by Mr. Schiller.

ACTIVE:
Mr. Schiller baked this bread.

PASSIVE:
In the scene it was proved that Gatsby was innocent.

ACTIVE:
The scene proved Gatsby innocent.

As you can see, sometimes one fatty usage leads to another—in this case, a sagging *it* developed a passive verb, which led to a lazy *was.*

One warning about all this butchering. You can't always cut out an *is,* or a *which,* or a *there.* These words have their uses. "It is hot," for example—two empty calories out of three—can't really be tightened or improved. The same is true of the passive voice—a writer will now and then use it purposefully, as Russell Baker does on page 129. When Baker writes, "Kerosene lamps were cleaned and polished," the passive expresses a child's feeling of distance from grown-up chores, as if they somehow get done magically without a *doer.*

Writing isn't a matter of rule, but of taste. Read, write, and ruthlessly edit, and you won't mistake fat for good meat.

CORRECT DOESN'T COUNT

When you trim the fat, you're strengthening, not correcting. No grammar book would complain of "the keys become stiff or sticky." It's correct, but that doesn't make it good. Many people write empty, deceitful prose that is perfectly "correct." But many people don't get in to First Choice University. Think about what you're trying to say and *don't be concerned about correctness.*

Why not? Because admissions officers—not being editors or English teachers—don't know or care much about the fine points of grammar. Most admissions officers wouldn't know which is correct:

A. Chris is one of those reporters who always meets his deadline.
B. Chris is one of those reporters who always meet their deadlines.

Even admissions readers who *do* know can't pause long enough to think about it, and it doesn't make much difference. (B is correct; "who" refers to reporters, not Chris.)

I don't mean throw grammar and punctuation out the window. Just don't *think* about it. Unless you have problems with the basics—periods at the end of sentences, subject-verb agreement—it's not an issue. By senior year you know enough grammar to write a college essay. Use what you're familiar with and don't get fancy. Concentrate on the writing.

Spelling is different. I've seen otherwise intelligent admissions officers get themselves into a lather about student spelling, as if it mattered. (Usually because the applicant misspelled the name of the college.) Spelling is a *visual* skill that has nothing to do with intelligence. Either you can spell or you can't spell. Many great writers can't. Many admissions officers can. Solution: give your essay to a good speller when you're finished. And follow the same principle if you can't help worrying about the grammar: give it to someone who's good at it.

Neatness also counts. If your handwriting looks like mashed insects, type your essay. If the college instructs you to write in your own hand, as Brown does, print carefully or send a typed translation as well.

But even so, remember that one typo or spelling error won't sink you. One empty idea, vaguely developed, will.

TAKING THE TIME TO BE SHORT

As you may be beginning to see, it takes time to simplify. If I plan a week in advance to drive to French Lick, Indiana, I will probably consult a map and take the shortest route. But if I must leave *now*, with no time to plot a course, I'll probably get lost or go the long way around. It takes time—and effort—to be quick.

I'm going to start with the assumption that you're a Last-Minute Louie (or Louise). I, too, am one. I know people who prepare for weeks—outlining, sharpening pencils like mad, and stacking up neat piles of paper—and finish days ahead of schedule. They are beneath contempt. But because I am so slow, I know the lengths you have to go to leave yourself enough time at the end to be ruthless in revision. If you know you're a deadline dawdler, set yourself an artificial limit way ahead of your actual schedule: tell a friend or a teacher or whoever's serving as your reader that you'll have a polished final draft ready to read a week before your mailing date. This sounds silly and transparent, but it works—you'll usually miss your phony deadline too, but not by much, and then you'll have three or four days to mull over your final draft and buff it to a high sheen.

You must figure into your schedule a time to put your essay away for a day or two when you have finished a complete draft. Getting away from it allows you to come back with fresh eyes. Weaknesses you missed before suddenly cry out, and new ideas arrive for transitions, for endings, for refining the lead. The shape of the whole and the details are visible when you can look at them as if for the first time.

Taking time also helps you be ruthless. The writer of the bathroom essay cut this paragraph, originally the fourth in the piece, entirely:

> I'm not sure I know why it happens, but it works in almost any bathroom, though ones with windows are especially good. I have to admit the bathroom is a strange place for inspiration. Most people don't want to think about the bathroom, something you can tell from the dishonest name we've given it. (I've seen plenty of bathrooms without bathtubs and even showers, but never one without a toilet.)

Why not call it the "toiletroom," to be accurate? Or something upbeat like SaniRama? My little brother calls it "baffroom," a good name. It sounds like a fast-car noise in a cartoon.

It's a good paragraph. It's funny, and it says something. The writer worked hard on it and never thought about doing without it. Then, after putting the essay away, he had two problems: 1) he saw this paragraph as a digression, and 2) the whole essay was too long. So the paragraph had to go.

What is too long? Although some colleges limit the number of words, please be assured that they do not employ a brood of monks to count them. It's that extra page that makes the difference. Work to fit yours onto one side of a sheet (single spaced, if typed). Some schools confine you to a particular space, in which case your mission is clear. But for colleges without space or word requirements, or who simply use the ominous term "brief," what is too long? Keep to a page. If you absolutely *must* go on—and I don't see why you must—make sure you're into your concluding cadences by the time the admissions officer turns the page. Use your head about this. On the Princeton application, for instance, the essay begins about halfway down the page; you *have* to attach a separate sheet. But halfway down that second sheet is far enough. *Never, ever should an essay be three pages.*

But now let's look at what all this rewriting and editing does for an essay, from notes to final draft.

9 Evolution of an Essay

One college requests, "Please share with us what you believe other students would learn from you, both inside and outside the classroom."

Tough assignment. The temptation to pretend to be something you're not, or to recite your accomplishments, is almost overwhelming. What can you say? "I hope other students will learn from me the values of hard work and fun as well." Ugh. It leads easily to the Jock or the 3D essay. One young woman, knowing the traps buried in the assignment, began by leafing through her notebook. She came across an entry:

> My sister is a kick. Seven years old, and she's the only one who knows how to run the VCR. So now she wants one of her own for Christmas. Whatever happened to AM-FM radio for kids? At her age I thought fiddling around with the wires to get a clear picture on the Brady Bunch was pretty good. Mom is out of it, can't even deal with cable, can't get her radio to work without static. Sister's already working on computers in school. I feel bad for Mom—some of the stuff even I can't figure out. New technology is fine, I guess, given the fact that I like old movies on the VCR too, but there has to be something else. What? I don't know. Bike trips?

Using this as a starting point, she wrote a draft:

> When I asked my seven-year-old sister what she wanted for Christmas last year, her answer was short, simple and automatic. "Uh . . . Get-In-Shape-Girls, My Little Pony and a VCR."

I can remember the days (and hey—that's not so long ago) when it was crazy for kids to want even a cassette recorder. AM-FM radio was about as far as any of us got. As for television, I used to think I was a big shot because I knew just which wire to twist to erase the fuzzy-static sound that was forever drowning out the entire Brady Bunch. But now my seven-year-old sister is the one who teaches the rest of us about the latest technology. She is official keeper of the VCR. That's because she's the only one who *really* knows how to make it do all the things it's designed to. Mom, meanwhile, still can't tune in her favorite radio station on our Casio Supreme Stereo, and she's helpless when faced with the mesmerizing, ominous "Cable Box." A few months ago I watched my sister try to show Mom which buttons to push to record a TV show that would be on later that day. The generation gap is getting wider in our house, byte by byte, chip by chip.

So one of the things my future classmates will not be learning from me is how to adjust to changes in home entertainment. They'll have to see my sister for that. I'm just too old to understand.

I've also learned a few other things from my sister. Last summer we flew from New York to London in only six hours, which didn't make much of an impression on my sister. She didn't understand why it took so *long*. From my point of view, the ride was a far cry from spectacular; the cabin was cramped, the wallpaper and seat coverings were dizzying, the air was clogged by the stench of old sneakers and formaldehyde, the food (?) was disgusting, and somewhere along the line I lost five hours of my life. Where that time went I'll never understand, but at least it had the decency to come back four weeks later, upon my return home.

When she had gotten this far, the writer stopped to ask, Where am I? She originally wanted to say she hoped other students might learn from her how much fun bike trips and the outdoors could be, as opposed to the kind of prepackaged entertainment she saw around her all the time. Anyway, she knew she had nothing against the VCR—she liked it in fact. But in avoiding the dumb sounding "I hope people learn from me that bike trips are fun," she had gotten off the track, writing about her sister and their different attitudes. She was not getting very quickly to what other students would learn from her in college. Where did this airplane business lead? She could start revising sections now—that would be one way to try to pick up the thread of the main idea—but it was too soon for that. Since she was rolling along toward her bike story, she decided to get it out and see where it led:

> I have also ridden a bicycle across Canada, 750 miles in 28 days, during which time it rained for two weeks straight. Needless to say, I learned to appreciate the sun. As it happens, I also learned to enjoy the rain. My journey was slow, yes. But it was refreshing (there is a small brook in Algonquin Park with water so cold it could chill a penguin), informative (an old man in Whitney Ontario will tell you more about trout fishing than you'll ever want to know), and far more beautiful (from the soft evergreens lining Fodder Pond to the hard cobblestone streets in Old Quebec) than any voyage through darkness in an oblong metal box could ever hope to be.
>
> I am no naturalist; I don't eat bark. I like junk food as much as the next person, and I am the first to run to the video shop when my family wants a movie for that VCR. But I have discovered along the way that one thing does not have to exclude the other. I can only teach people that which I myself have already learned. And I would take pride in showing someone first hand that popcorn tastes just as good while you're watching a sunset from a mountaintop as it does while you're watching an old movie.

This draft has many merits. The writer has observed carefully and much of the writing is alive. But it's not coherent—it's like two different essays, one about TV and VCRs and technology, the other about learning and teaching and her family. But she knew she didn't have time for two different essays. She tried to find ways to connect them, or cut one out, which meant thinking about the lead and the end, and what the connection might be. She was thinking of shape.

The end seemed fine for the time being. But the lead, even

though it was anecdotal, didn't lead anywhere. She cut the original opening and tried a few new ones:

> I used to think I was a big shot because I knew just which wire to twist to erase the fuzzy-static sound that was forever drowning out the entire Brady Bunch.

Or:

> There are a few things my classmates *won't* learn from me.

She thought the last one was good because it got into the teaching and learning idea—the point of the assignment, after all—quickly. A little negative, though. She hunted in her ending for another lead that might do the trick differently: "I can only teach that which I myself have already learned." And seeing this line, she couldn't help improving it: "I can only teach what I have already learned."

Then, thinking of her sister again, she added: ". . . which seems to be shrinking compared to what everyone else knows."

She tried keeping the learning idea but starting with her sister:

> In my life I have many teachers and a mother who likes to lecture, but it's my sister, age seven, who does most of the teaching.

Working on the lead made her start to understand what her essay might be about. And thinking of her sister at the beginning made her think of the ending, and how far away she had gotten from her sister. She liked writing about her sister and thought it would be good to shape the essay around her, if possible. But how to get back to her? The writer changed the last line to:

> And I would take pride in showing someone (maybe even my sister when she's old enough) first hand that popcorn tastes just as good while you're watching a sunset from a mountaintop as it does while you're watching an old movie.

Something good was beginning to happen. But she also worried about the middle of the essay. The travel stories wandered. Could she find something in the beginning and the end that might bind the middle? Young sister, the writer feeling so old by comparison, technology, movies, popcorn, teaching and learning?

Seeing the vague "other things" in the first sentence of the airplane paragraph, she changed it to:

> I've also learned how to take other technology for granted from my sister.

And at the end of that paragraph, picking up on the time idea:

> I wondered if I kept flying east, would I get younger and younger (and eventually understand things)?

That was a funny idea—that people might actually know less and less as they approached twenty-one. It wasn't serious, of course, but it might be a good connection to what her sister and maybe her classmates could learn from her—an idea she was already trying to bring out at the end.

Then she thought of beginning the next-to-last paragraph with this:

> Without my sister, I have also ridden . . .

Which quickly developed into:

> There are a few things I haven't been too old to learn on my own, though. While my sister went to camp, I rode a bicycle . . .

Where was all this going? Did she have a main idea? She tried stating it: "Someone might learn from me that there are things worth more than the latest gadget." But it wasn't that bike trips were *worth* more than VCRs. Maybe, "Someone might learn from me about pleasures at least as satisfying as the latest gadget." Or something like that. She'd come back to it.

Now, with her destination getting clearer, she hoped honing some sentences would make the whole idea sharper in her mind. Already she had changed "fuzzy static sound" to "static." She substituted the single, exact "alien" for the two words "mesmerizing, ominous," as well as "widening" for "getting wider." (Weak use of "get"; remember?) She deleted "that would be on later that day" as unnecessary. She also changed "upon my return" (too formal) to "when we flew home," and "during which time" to "when." If it really was "needless to say," she didn't need to say it, and "as it happens" was just conversational filler; the piece did not lose its friendly tone without them. The stench "of" old sneakers and formaldehyde was wrong. (Although a few old sneakers might have found their way on board, formaldehyde probably hadn't.) She changed "of" to "like," creating the simile she had intended in the first place.

Here's the first rewrite. (She added the brackets around trouble spots afterward.)

Though I have many teachers and a mom who likes to lecture, in my life it's my sister, age seven, who does most of the instructing. After all, she's the only one who really knows how to make the VCR do everything it's designed to. I used to think I was a big shot when I was her age because I knew just which wire to twist to erase the fuzzy-static [that was forever drowning out] the Brady Bunch. My mom still can't tune in her favorite radio station on our Casio Supreme Stereo, and she's helpless when faced with the alien cable box. A few months ago I watched my sister try to show her which buttons to push to record a TV show. Poor Mom—the generation gap is widening in our house, byte by byte, chip by chip.

I've also learned to take other technology for granted from my sister. Last summer we flew from New York to London in only six hours, [which] didn't impress her much. She didn't understand why it took so *long*. (There's nothing more jaded than a seven-year-old.) [From my point of view], the ride was [a far cry] from spectacular; the cabin was cramped, the wallpaper and seat coverings were dizzying, the air was clogged by a stench like old sneakers and formaldehyde, the food (?) was disgusting, and [somewhere along the line] I lost five hours of my life. Where that time went I'll never understand, but at least it had the decency to come back four weeks later when we flew home. What would have happened if I kept flying east? Would I get younger and younger (and eventually understand things)?

[There are] a few [things] I haven't been too old to learn on my own, though. While my sister went to camp, I

rode a bicycle across Canada, 750 miles in 28 days, when it
rained for two weeks straight. I learned to appreciate the
sun, but I also learned to enjoy the rain. My journey was
slow, yes. But it was refreshing ([there is] a small brook in
Algonquin Park with water so cold it could chill a penguin)
informative (an old man in Whitney Ontario [will tell you]
more about trout fishing than [you'll ever want to know]),
and far more beautiful (from the soft evergreens lining
Fodder Pond to the hard cobblestone streets in Old Quebec)
than any voyage through darkness in an oblong metal box
[could ever hope to be.]

I am no naturalist; I don't eat bark. I like junk food as
much as the next person, and I am the first to run to the
video shop when my family wants a movie for that VCR.
But I have discovered [along the way] that one [thing] does
not have to exclude the other. I can only teach people what
I have already learned. And I would take pride in showing
someone (maybe even my sister when she's old enough) first
hand that popcorn tastes just as good while you're watching
a sunset from a mountaintop as it does while you're
watching an old movie.

At this point, the lead still wasn't right, and she didn't have the
solution to the problem of the end. She decided now was a good
time to put it away for a while.

Two days later, looking at it fresh, she rewrote the lead and
the last paragraph where most of the trouble was, three more
times, grinding slowly to get the ideas right. The end had to tie
it all together, and it didn't yet.

She didn't really like the assignment very much, and she
wanted the ending to reflect the honest humility she felt about it.
In the beginning she had tried, in a light way, to say that she didn't
like to teach. She liked learning from example, and from doing
things. So she decided to change "take pride in showing someone," because it sounded so teachy. It took most of a Saturday
afternoon to finish.

I think my classmates might learn more from my sister.
She's seven. I'm not much of a teacher, and neither is my
mom, though like a lot of moms she likes to lecture. But

around here my sister, who doesn't even know how to lecture, does most of the instructing. After all, she's the only one who really can make the VCR do everything it's designed to. I used to think I was a big shot when I was her age because I knew just which wire to twist to erase the static drowning out the Brady Bunch. Mom is even worse than I am—she still can't tune in her favorite radio station on our Casio Supreme, and she's helpless when faced with the alien cable box, never mind the VCR. A few months ago I watched my sister try to show her which buttons to push to record a TV show. Poor Mom—the generation gap is widening in our house, byte by byte, chip by chip.

My sister has also taught me how to take other inventions in stride. Last summer we flew from New York to London in only six hours. My sister wasn't impressed. She didn't understand why it took so *long*. (There's nothing more jaded than a seven-year-old.) I tried to be blasé too, but it wasn't easy. The cabin was cramped, the wallpaper and seat coverings were dizzying, the air was clogged by a stench like old sneakers and formaldehyde, the food was disgusting, and I lost five hours of my life. Where that time went I'll never understand, but at least it had the decency to come back four weeks later when we flew home. What would have happened if I kept flying east? Would I get younger and younger (and eventually be seven and finally Understand Things)?

There are a few lessons I haven't been too old to learn on my own, though. While my sister went to camp that same summer, I rode a bicycle across Canada with ten other people, 750 miles in twenty-eight days. It rained for two weeks straight. Needless to say, I learned to appreciate the sun. I also learned to enjoy the rain. My journey was slow but refreshing (a small brook in Algonquin Park runs so cold it could chill a penguin), informative (an old man in Whitney, Ontario, told me more about trout fishing than I can remember), and far more beautiful (from the soft evergreens lining Fodder Pond to the hard cobblestone streets in Old Quebec) than any high speed voyage through darkness in an oblong metal box.

But I'm no bark-munching naturalist. In fact, I eat as much popcorn as the next person, who happens to be my sister, the popcorn queen. And I'm always feeding that same VCR an old movie to have with my popcorn. I live in both these worlds, my sister's up-to-the-minute New York and the slower satisfactions of bike trips through the country. I don't know if anyone could learn something from that combination, though it's pretty important to me. But someone—maybe even my sister, when she's no longer young enough to know everything—might find out from me first hand that popcorn tastes just as good while you're watching a sunset from a mountaintop as it does while you're watching *Gone With the Wind*. Maybe even better.

It's impossible to show every change, every rejected phrase—that would require another whole book—but I hope you get an idea of the distance an essay must travel before it's ready to make the final trip to the admissions office.

Next I want to suggest a few ways to stretch one essay idea across many of the sometimes bizarre questions colleges ask.

READING

10 The Questions

There's no getting around it—you'll have to write more than one essay. A single application, like the University of Pennsylvania's, can ask for two or more. But you don't want to write twelve. With a little juggling, you should be able to limit your agonies.

Essay topics (not all of them are questions) come in two basic types: Generals and Specials. The Generals are the "Write anything you want" essays, but Specials zero in on a specific idea in an attempt to force students beyond dull warbling about themselves and their accomplishments. But both Specials and Generals are asking for a *personal statement*. Don't be fooled by a Special into writing something dry and academic.

Many colleges allow you to choose among a General and a few Specials. Step one in giving yourself a break begins when you assemble all your applications in the fall and do a little analysis of the essay questions. You should be trying to *reduce the number of Specials* to the absolute minimum or, when there's no getting around them, choosing Specials that a General will fit. For instance, let's suppose five out of six of your application essays are Generals: "Tell us anything," "Write about a topic of your choice," etc. The sixth, which you can't duck, is "Please discuss something you have read that has a special significance for you." You are going to write that sixth essay so that it can serve for all your Generals as well. "Something you have read," remember, not necessarily a *book*. It could be an advertisement, a newspaper headline you saw once, the first thing you remember reading, a letter from a friend, a cereal box—anything. If you have gotten this far, you know that every essay you write should carry a personal stamp, no matter what the topic.

Many of the colleges know each others' questions, so you have to be careful. It's not wise to submit a "The person I'd like to interview" essay as your personal statement to Yale, for instance. They immediately smell Penn in that.

But there are also ways to alter one essay to make it suit a few different topics. I'll try to fit the bathroom essay to a few to show you what I mean.

I've picked a few essay topics from the applications of some of the most competitive schools in the country. Colleges often change their questions from year to year, but they rarely change the *type* of question they ask. You'll find most of the old favorites below, but if you're applying to a place that asks "What kind of vegetable would you like to be, and why?" you're going to have to answer that question specifically. And good luck to you.

(Note: The "optional essay"—the one the college says you don't have to write if you think the rest of your file represents you well enough—is not optional. Write the essay.)

Let's begin by comparing two very different topics from two very competitive schools.

The University of Pennsylvania, which requires two different essays, is as full of Specials as a Hammacher Schlemmer catalog:

> 1. On a separate sheet of paper please answer one of the following two questions in an essay not to exceed three hundred words. We are interested not so much in whom or what you choose to write about, but in how you use your choice to illustrate something important about yourself and your values.
>
> > A. If you were given the opportunity to spend an evening with any one person, living, deceased or fictional, whom would you choose and why?
> >
> > B. Please cite and discuss a literary quotation or brief passage that has special meaning to you.
>
> 2. While we are very interested in your intellectual abilities, your sense of imagination and creativity are also important to us. With this in mind, please respond to one of the following two requests.

A. You have just completed your 300 page autobiography. Please submit page 217.

B. Create something on or with an 8 and a half by 11 inch piece of paper or other thin, flat material. All means of expression, written or otherwise, are equally encouraged. (You must be able to mail this in a 10" × 13" envelope.)

What to make of all this? The questions a school asks tell a great deal about what they value. Penn is trying to encourage the "creative" response—note how they phrase even the simple request for a General (2 A). They are more than just weary and wary of the same old essays—they want to be entertained. These are good-time people.

Compare the University of Chicago essay:

Please respond to ONE of the following questions.

1. The word "hero" is loosely used to describe a wide array of human beings. The writers of ancient Greece used the word only to honor warriors who sought glory on the battlefield. Today, we acclaim as "heroes" such varied kinds of people as astronauts, firefighters, athletes, movie stars, and ordinary citizens caught in extraordinary situations. Are we correct in using the term so broadly? Give an example of a real or fictional person you consider a hero and discuss what makes that person heroic.

2. Concepts and feelings are sometimes represented by common household items. For example, the theory of an expanding universe is sometimes portrayed in terms of raisin bread rising, or love as a red, red rose. Illustrate how an object in your kitchen can be used to represent a significant concept or feeling. (Feel free to discuss more than one object.)

3. The Constitution is conspicuously silent about matters of education. For example, the only requirements for elected office are citizenship and a certain age level (Article I, Sections 2, 3; Article I, Section 1). Is there any kind of knowledge or understanding most worth having for a good citizen who wishes to hold elected office?

4. Discuss some creative work that has been crucial to the way you see the world and the way you see yourself in the world. Name the work and tell us its effect on you. Keep in

mind that such works of art may include novels, films, poems, scientific theories, biographies, and other diverse forms.

We encourage you to have fun with your answer. You need not write at length or use elevated language. We are primarily concerned with your ability to reason, to think creatively, and to write clearly and accurately.

Have *fun?* What you get from these questions is that this place considers itself *serious.* (Compare to Penn's happy-go-lucky 2 B.) The whole thing reads like an exam. Ancient Greece! Articles of the Constitution! Expanding universe! Even the length of the questions shows the cap and gown poking out from under their casual admissions getup. (In academia, no question is good unless it's at least half as long as the answer.)

I don't mean to pick on Penn and Chicago, but you can see how difficult it can sometimes be to keep your essays to a minimum. If you had already written the bathroom essay, there's not much you can do to squeeze it into Chicago's questions. But at Penn, you could easily tailor it to suit 2A:

> I do some of my best thinking in the bathroom. I don't mean to upset anyone by talking about something so personal, but it's been true ever since I was in high school, and I suspect it's true of a lot of people who don't acknowledge it.
> I remember when I began to see I wasn't the only one . . .

Then you would change into past tense all the verbs until the next-to-last paragraph, which can stay in the present. "Dad" would become "my father": "I got my start in the bathroom, like most of us, from my father. He used to call it the reading room. He thought he was joking, but I noticed that for years the bathroom was actually the only place he read anything." Any good personal statement could be altered like this. It beats writing another one.

Generals are by far the most common request, and for questions like the ones below you can use the identical essay:

> You may choose ANY topic about which you would like to write. (Harvard.)

What would you most like the Admissions Committee to know about you when reading your application? (Georgetown)

An autobiographical statement of 200–400 words. (Bryn Mawr)

Please use the space on the back to let us know something about you that we might not learn from the rest of the application. (Yale)

Use this page to give a description of yourself. (Columbia)

A special interest, experience, achievement, or anything else you would like us to know about you. (Hamilton)

Why not, then, use this opportunity to tell us about anything you think we should know. (Brown)

We would like you to write an essay on any topic that is of *genuine interest to you.* (Emory)

We invite you to reflect on an issue or experience that is significant to you or to your perspective on the world around you. (Princeton)

Use the essay to tell about yourself. (University of California, all campuses)

Among Specials, a few recur:

1. Discuss an issue of personal, local, or national concern and its importance to you.

2. Please describe in detail a personal interest, experience, or accomplishment of importance to you. (Williams College rephrases it, "Comment on an experience that helped you to discern or define a value that you hold.")

3. Describe the greatest challenge you have faced or expect to face. (Hamilton calls it "The most difficult thing you have ever done.")

4. Identify a person who has had a significant influence on you and describe that influence. (Wesleyan)

But numbers one and two, in using "personal," give you a clear opening for your General essay. The bathroom essay would fit those questions perfectly well, as would the frustrated cowgirl (p. 113) or "Only at Night" (p. 108), or any of the other personal statements. They wouldn't even need alterations.

Williams calls their request a Personal Statement, and it contains elements of both General and Special. "Comment on an experience that helped you to discern or define a value that you hold." An *experience*—sounds pretty specific. Not a personal interest, not a book, not someone. But with a quick new lead, the bathroom essay goes off to Williams too:

> I'd like to comment, not on one experience, but on a continuing series of them. You see, I do some of my best thinking in the bathroom.

Sometimes you can write one essay for two Specials. Stanford asks you to "Select your favorite quotation, or one that holds special importance for you, and comment on its significance." One of Amherst's two assignments: "In the course of your high school education, you have encountered simple and complex concepts, challenging ideas, profound thought and art in many forms. Please describe one or more of those encounters and your reflections on it or them."

You can use the Stanford essay for both of these, since an essay about a quotation easily counts as a "reflection" on an "encounter" with "challenging ideas, profound thought."

Some Specials, of course, you'll have to address, like Wesleyan's "Please share with us what you believe other Wesleyan students would learn from you, both inside and outside the classroom," or their "Identify a person who has had a significant influence on you and describe that influence," both required. Approach your Specials the same way you would a General, by making a personal statement—simple, vivid, detailed, close to what you know.

SHORT TAKES

Throughout this book I have concentrated on the 200–500-word essay, but now and then I am asked about how to handle the short questions, like "Which activity has benefited you most?" Typically colleges allot only an inch or two for the answer, but some will leave space for a paragraph. Here are some typical short takes:

Write a brief statement describing your academic goals.

Write a brief statement describing one or two non-academic activities you would most like to pursue in college.

Describe the most enriching academic or intellectual experience you have had.

Briefly describe why you think First Choice is a good place for you to be a student.

Because you must answer these in two or three inches of space at most—under 100 words in every case—you can't build up a head of steam, but you don't have to chug like a freight train, either. You can always say something worthwhile:

> It may not qualify as academic, though it was certainly enriching: Dr. Seuss's *On Beyond Zebra*, the first book I read on my own, showed me reading could be more than Dick and Jane. It could be fun.

Concise and unpretentious. Be straight and simple, but be honest and give a detail, too. You can imagine the clichés of the short answers. Why would First Choice be a good place for you? "First Choice has a world-renowned faculty and fine students and facilities, and I feel confident I could reach my true potential there." Blagh. That's *bad* b.s. Much better: "When I visited in November I met people in East Dorm who took me to a jazz concert and stayed up half the night arguing about the apartheid demonstration on campus. I decided I wanted to spend some time here."

If you want to go to First Choice only because it *is* First Choice—the prestige factor—you won't be able to answer the question without thoughtless and empty phrases. Even if you are originally attracted to a college only because it "has a name," you'd better do some investigating on your own. In the admissions brochures, every place looks the same—terrific.

What's true of the long essays is true of the short—the more you know, the better you'll write.

11 Exhibits: The Quick and the Dull

Here are a few student essays to help sharpen your judgment. As you read each one, ask yourself what you learn about the writer, and whether you like the person you see.

I have asked a small group of current and former admissions officers—Lifers and Temps from a few of the nation's most selective colleges—to respond to them exactly as they would in reading applications. They saw only what you see below, the essays themselves—no other parts of the applications. Evaluating the essays out of their usual context is tricky, but in most cases it didn't seem to bother my panelists; what you hear from them is a good sampling of backstage admissions talk. In order to allow them to speak so freely, they are identified only by number after each essay. In some cases I've added a postscript to clarify their readings.

Remember that this is only a sampling. Like many other admissions officers, my panelists have strong opinions that are sometimes unreasonable. For instance, many admissions officers dislike essays about the application process itself, which they feel shows an unappealing "sweatiness." In other words, colleges are glad to be extremely selective, but they don't like it when you are aware of that. They want you to act as if pressure, or even the application itself, doesn't exist, and that the whole process is simply a nice chat between you and them.

You may also notice that they love to play amateur psychologist. It's an occupational hazard.

But the most important lesson here is seeing how often

admissions people disagree. Different readers, even in the same admissions office, look for different things. I remember epic battles with admissions colleagues over whether an essay showed a student was a potential scholar or just a nerd, a future physicist or just a pre-med. How can you please them? You can't. Say what *you* have to say. The exact same essay, slipped into the folders of two different students with comparable academic credentials, might lead to different results. Essay (F), didn't prevent the writer, a Just Folks applicant, from being admitted to one of the two or three most selective colleges in the country, despite the outrage of my panelists. This chapter, above all, will show how senseless it is to ask, "What are they looking for?" They—as a group, as a college—don't always know themselves.

(A) Describe the greatest challenge you have faced or expect to face.

Except for my struggle with jacks—I could never get past sixies while Leslie Ackerman whizzed through tenzies and back to onezies all in one turn—this application is the greatest challenge I've faced. I'm glad you didn't ask how I dealt with it.

I hope I'm not dodging or taking the easy way out. It's hard to find an honest answer to your question. Nothing I've done so far could be called a "great challenge." A minor annoyance, maybe: there was my brush with Physics, when I tried to understand the practical results of impractical problems, like where an iron ball will land if thrown out of a moving car. (When I brought up in class that I never *would* throw an iron ball out of a moving car, Mr. Weitz just looked at me.) Before that came the separate trials of learning the Australian crawl and the slice backhand, the first for water survival and the second, my parents said, for social survival. And, of course, the intensely competitive jacks. (At age nine, to be the best jacks player was also to be the most popular girl.) All these experiences were difficult—getting anything right in tennis still seems more like a miracle—but I can't imagine calling one of them my "greatest challenge."

Challenge seems like it should be something bigger, and I'm not sure I've faced it yet. I've never had to work to support my family, as my mother did when she was my age. Unlike my older brother, I've never had to find an affordable apartment in New York City. I've never even experienced what some of my New Jersey friends say is the greatest challenge of all—fighting the 8:00 A.M. traffic on the George Washington Bridge, unsure if they'll ever get to school. I live in Manhattan, which, now that I think about it, may be challenge enough for anyone. But that's probably not what you had in mind.

Putting together these forms for you, on the other hand, comes closer to what I think of as "challenge." That may be only because I want to go to Dartmouth more than I ever wanted to imitate Chris Evert Lloyd. But part of the challenge has to do with what applying to college means—writing essays, remembering teachers and classes and sports, answering questions, all this self examination. At least in physics problems there was always a formula to plug in. But there are no "correct" answers, everybody keeps telling me, on the application; there's not even a correct method, where you can get points for reaching the wrong answer the right way. There's only me. It's a serious challenge, if not a great one, to distill on four sides of blue paper the person I've become in seventeen years. It's like trying to put myself into a little jar—a jar of Justine—and yet somehow hoping that I won't fit, that I can't be categorized. The whole thing makes sevenzies look easy.

1. I usually dislike essays about how hard the process is (which is what they must get nine out of ten times in response to this question), but at least this has a warm, funny tone to it that's appealing. Don't learn much about the kid, though.

2. (This is a *dumb* question—part of the reason her answer is so weak. She's never faced, at seventeen or eighteen, a real challenge. If she has faced one, she hasn't got enough perspective to know it.) However—to her response: Useless! I have no interest in her anxiety about the college process. All I learn from this is that she'd be overcome if she ever faced a *significant* challenge.

3. Too pat and attempts to be cute and humorous. Much of the essay seems addressed to the admissions committee in an overly self-conscious way. The clever trick doesn't work here.

4. Breezy, savvy, lighthearted but well-written essay.

Sometimes you have to put up with a college's essay assignment. Although she wrote about applying—a no-no, usually—the result is a good piece. Two admissions officers for, two against.

(B) Comment on an experience that helped you discern or define a value you hold.

In the primaries of the presidential election in 1984, Rev. Jesse Jackson ran for the Democratic nomination without the backing of major party officials. But, even knowing his efforts would be in vain, Jackson continued to make his voice heard.

While high school elections may not have the wide significance of national primaries, I believe I encountered a similar situation this fall in running for Student Body President without the backing of the most popular seniors. Although the outcome of that election was a setback, the gratification I received from defending my beliefs made the attempt worthwhile.

From the start I planned a campaign that would focus on issues, not personalities. Also, unlike the other two candidates, I had little support and thus had to design and execute campaign posters, slogans, and my platform without assistance. These tasks were time-consuming and forced me to adopt a more organized and self-disciplined manner in order to continue to achieve my goals: first, to enhance the atmosphere of the school through public awareness of issues; and second, to impact the maximum audience with my concepts.

Though the election was destined to become simply a popularity contest, I was determined to stand by my convictions. When one of the individuals involved in the election refused to enter into a debate with me on key issues, I wrote a letter which was published in the town newspaper. Many of my peers disagreed with this action and with my views, but my primary concern was to stimulate discussion and make it evident I was a serious candidate. I believe I accomplished this purpose in the face of considerable opposition.

A few students did express their agreement with my

positions, but there was great pressure throughout the campaign to make empty promises of improved social life or a more forceful stance on the part of students toward the administration. I knew that my stressing more constructive issues cost me much support; one or two of my friends wondered why I spent so much time in organizational and promotional efforts if I wasn't trying to win votes. I certainly wanted the support of my peers, but I could only tell them that I had to say what I thought was right, regardless of outcome.

Though my campaign was unsuccessful and often frustrating, I learned a great deal from it, perhaps more than if I'd won. I found that in terms of self motivation I am capable of an inner strength that allows me to accomplish my goals, even while I'm facing difficulties and anxieties. Even more crucial was an understanding of the value of sticking to one's beliefs, even if they are not shared by a majority. Afterward, I could look back with pride on the positions I represented.

It's possible that someday I may have to take other unpopular positions, but I can look forward to such a situation, knowing I can maintain my integrity in the face of peer pressure.

1. And blah, blah, blah. The campaign—organized and self-disciplined—was probably, like the essay, dull as dishwater. This is a real nit in the making.

2. I'm not especially impressed. It's all there, all correct, but a bit self-serving for my taste. Perhaps it's just healthy confidence. Do the grades and teacher recommendations warrant the benefit of the doubt? Ultimately, not my type.

3. The stance here is obnoxiously self-congratulatory. Candidate comes off as self-centered and the writing is awkward. Passive voice employed much too often.

4. Rather dry essay portraying a determined, apparently principled young person. Hard working, etc.

The piece is full of empty buzzing, like "maintain my integrity" and "impact the maximum audience with my concepts." It's basically a Jock essay—through school politics I learned integrity.

(C) Describe a person who has influenced you.

MR. SOMARY

I have always wanted to take his picture there in rehearsal, when he stands in the middle of a semicircle of upturned eyes and open mouths, grandiosely waving his endless arms as though he were swimming through the music. At eight-thirty in the morning, when the rest of us are barely awake, Johannes Somary is at his lovable best. The sun opposite me shines on the sopranos and altos and silhouettes his aristocratic nose, shaggy brows and frizz of hair against the window pane and the morning sky.

"Rrrroll your R's!" he says. Then he stomps and wiggles, bellows and whispers, puts his fingers to his chin as if in prayer and opens his blue eyes so wide they seem to leap out directly into mine, to discover that mine are closed; I am nodding asleep to the march rhythms of Handel's Mass in Time of War. But not for long. He goes through every conceivable contortion and exertion to energize our eighty sleepy faces. It is as if his wild gestures could conduct electricity as well as music through the drowsy air into our voices. Sometimes I wonder what he would do if we returned in kind, bugging our eyes out, wriggling and twisting our bodies to the music. As it is, we continue to hold our notes too long or not long enough and we refuse to "dance" with the 3/4 time.

Every once in a while he launches into a boiling tirade—he "Swisses out." Then he reverts to European discipline: "If not every person is in this room at exactly eighteen minutes past eight o'clock, there will be no concert." He is the quintessential Swiss in other ways as well: we must learn to speak English, not Americanese, we must not be "cool" when singing Haydn, we must get eight hours of sleep, be prompt, attentive, enunciate our consonants, and think about nothing else. This is the law according to Somary.

It works. His ridiculous energy and steaming rages do make us sit straighter, hold our scores higher and try a little harder. When he pleads, "Both feet on the floor—you cannot hope to sing if you do not support yourself," there is a second or two of shuffling and creaking as 160 legs are uncrossed. Then he spreads his own feet wide and arches his back a little, sticking out his pot belly and hitching up his belt. He's forever tucking in a stubborn shirt tail set free by quick tempi or forte passages. There is a lot of child in him. He can glower as furiously as a two-year-old when he says "Elephants have memories, people have pencils—write it down!" or he can smile so widely and coyly that I am afraid his grin will devour his ears and like Beethoven he will have to conduct from memory.

Of all my teachers, I feel the most loyalty to him because he devotes his entire self to his work. He does more than just wheedle a Haydn Mass out of us at a sleepy hour; his endless arm is as ready to wrap itself around my shoulder with a reassuring squeeze as it is to gyrate in 4/4 time, and he gives advice and drops of Somary-wisdom as freely as musical instruction. When he sits behind his messy desk after rehearsal and we sprawl—legs, arms, chatter, bookbags—on the couch in his comfortable office, he looks like a complacent Swiss Buddha, nodding and smiling those blue eyes at us, always there, always quirky, always inspiring to me.

1. Send it to *The New Yorker!* A more wonderful piece of description I've never read. The use of language and ability to convey mood is really remarkable. I'd love to have a kid who can write like this in the class.

2. Wonderful. I am the 81st choir member here. I am transported to Somary's rehearsal.

3. Excellent. I like the humor and descriptive quality of this essay. Good strong crisp writing.

4. Delightful and affectionate portrayal of choir director who inspires with his energy and commitment. Nice, warm piece.

(D) Tell us anything you think we should know.

The aspect of college I'm anticipating most is the chance to continue to refine my interpersonal skills. In high school I feel I have dedicated myself to academics and extracurriculars, but more especially I have enjoyed the contact with my peers in more informal settings such as the cafeteria or the moments between classes, when friends and acquaintances gather to talk about many subjects and ease the tensions of the school day. And yet high school is somewhat confining in this regard, as a result of spending so much scheduled time in class and, in my case, in being transported to and from school for over an hour each day. And yet working with people is often the key to success, as I have learned from the computer consulting company I formed with some friends last year. Of course we had to begin with a thorough knowledge of the subject, but the company taught us not only how to run a small business but also how to deal effectively with people—for instance, how to give customers information which is relevant to their questions. We also tutor both children and adults in using their computers, and I think that we have gained some helpful insights into teaching. I have learned that communication is just as important as knowledge, for, without the latter, the former is useless.

My work as assistant editor of the newspaper, a weekly that has won several awards for excellence from the Columbia Scholastic Press, also taught me the value of the personal touch. A good interview, for instance, demands revealing quotations from the subject. In interviewing people it is important to put them at ease before delving into their innermost feelings and ultimately obtaining valuable quotes; many stories unfortunately fall flat because the interviewer has not allowed his subject to relax. I have taken pride in my ability to get people to open up, resulting in a series of interviews that many have found revealing and readable.

In all my endeavors, I have discovered that knowing how to interact with many different varieties of people is invaluable. College, with its diverse social settings, its wide array of people, promises to provide the broad experience that gives education its special flavor. Having roommates from Ohio and Colorado and India can teach as much—maybe more!—than the best textbook or teacher. Although, through my interests in psychology, I plan to benefit academically from whatever college I attend, I am just as eager to benefit from the people I will meet in the course of four years.

1. I could have stopped after the first sentence. (After all, a good pickpocket has, in a sense, "refined his interpersonal

skills.") Anyway, we learn a couple of things about the writer, but the statement is poorly written and a dime a dozen.

2. I was getting interested in the computer company job, and then the gears switched. Too bad, because the momentum fizzled out, and is nothing by the end.

3. A walking cliché of an essay with bad grammar to boot. One almost gets ill.

4. Awkward, somewhat disjointed essay.

(E) Any topic.

ONLY AT NIGHT

The above is the title of a story I may someday write. Sordid romance? Spy mystery? Drug novel? Actually, it is a description of my work habits. To the horror of my parents, who are convinced they have brought up some kind of lunatic, I can concentrate only when the house is all mine. At three a.m., I rule the night.

Well, sort of. Unfortunately I cannot boast that I am someone well-adjusted to the night. My mother keeps a tally of the number of times she has opened my bedroom door to find me sprawled on the floor unconscious, buried in blue ink and American history. My appearance-conscious sister has often lectured me on the damaging social effects of dark circles under the eyes. Classes, which have a bad habit of taking place during the day, are often a blur. I don't wait for darkness because *Moby Dick* or trigonometric functions are any easier by night than by day; it's just that my work seems important, even vital, when I spend precious early morning hours doing it. My father thinks it is the result of too many suspense novels, but I don't know. If sneaking through the house for a bowl of Rice Krispies to keep me awake is the nearest I can come to fulfilling my fantasies of adventure and heroism, Robert Ludlum couldn't have had much of an effect.

Actually, adventure, if not heroism, has not always been that hard to come by. When I was six I would lie open-eyed in bed, waiting with terrified eagerness for a robber's creeping footsteps. I imagined myself bravely rescuing the entire family—that is, until one real creak from an upstairs floorboard would send me scurrying to my parents. But as I've grown older and my nocturnal vigils longer, my hopes of one day gaining the courage I would need in such a situation have only grown dimmer. I remember two exploits especially, one a midnight tramp through the jungles of Central Park with two friends who were searching for an obscure war monument; the other was a panicked call to the police to report a bomb I had seen smoking in the gateway of a sidestreet near my house. (It turned out to be a firecracker.) The park I survived by envisioning myself an undercover archeologist; the "bomb"—a daytime event—is now just a blur of tears and shaking.

The truth is I'm not really suited for night or day, but, responsibilities being what they are, you have to choose one. Though I've put a dent in my habit of classroom dozing with a strong brand of drip coffee, I still really work only in the dark hours of the morning, surrounded by my private goblins. Each to his own muse.

1. Give this person a single room. Humorous in spots and not a bad effort, I guess. But the second half falls off and though likable, he or she'd better have lots else going for him.

2. Be careful with roommate selection.

3. Not bad writing. Above average, but I don't think I got to know the candidate well. Many phrases meant to be clever fell short of their target.

4 Perhaps a bit overdone. Essay is fine but not unusual.

Here are the amateur shrinks. But this statement, with its variation on the Confession lead in the first paragraph, is a good one—notice the admissions officers seem to acknowledge that the writer will get in. (Otherwise there's no need to "be careful with roommate selection.") Their comments tell you how nitpicky they can be. The writer is at Harvard.

(F) Any topic.

NOTES FROM THE UNDERBRED
(with humblest apologies to Dostoevsky)

Gentlemen, you probably think I'm applying to your university out of some deep-felt love for the school and that

I'll jump up and down and cry if I get rejected. But I assure you that it's all the same to me. Really, gentlemen, I'd be much happier if you rejected me, for nothing would be more horrifying than to spend four years at your despicable institution. I'm joking, of course, and said this merely to shock you. Why, there's actually nothing more appetizing than the idea of spending four years at your holy and venerated institution—I visited there myself, and found the chess-playing facilities to be superb. But in fact, I don't play chess, and the one time I tried I ended up hurling the chessboard at my opponent. It was not the fact that he was constantly practicing psychological subtleties on me—no, his transparent tricks hardly bothered me at all. Rather, it was that this despicable and vain creature—whose name would be known to you gentlemen, if I would only mention it—simply sat there with a beatific smile on his face throughout the game, clasping his hands together and nodding every time I made a move. You laugh, of course, and wonder why that should torment me so. But it was abundantly clear at the time that he felt himself to be superior to me in all respects, not only that of chess, and nothing could have infuriated me more or been further from the truth, for I am actually quite a fine fellow.

Of course, gentlemen, you say to yourself, "I'll be the judge of that!" But in reality, who are you to judge who is a fine fellow and who isn't? You certainly have never met me, and in fact, I have no desire to meet you. For I find you and your occupation of reading essays to be entirely despicable. I say this to shock you again, of course, and to keep your attention, for I am assured by several authorities that all essay readers work at two o'clock in the morning with a six-pack of Heineken by their side. Does my saying this offend you? Gentlemen, I assure you that it is most certainly true! In fact, speaking for myself, I would do much the same if I were in your position, but each day I offer up a thousand thanks that I am not.

But I must stop now; I may be writing too many words. Of course, the very idea of limiting a person's essay to a predetermined length is absurd, for what if that person has something to say? He should be allowed to go on considerably longer, if not indefinitely. And who should be the judge of whether a person has something important to say? I am quite confident that I have something to say, but you probably disagree with me, especially since you are well into your second six-pack by now. Well reject me then, I assure you it's all the same to me. . . . I didn't mean that, of course.

1. Copycat. No, actually, he does a decent mimicry job here and he seems to have a mind that works well.

2. Did this person intentionally sabotage his application? This is easy—deny.

3. Sounds like this kid has written too many essays using downers. Terrible strategy with obvious death wish.

4. Tedious. The attempt at creativity falls flat. Says it's all the same to him if we reject him. We needn't disappoint him. We won't miss much if the essay's any indication of what he has to offer.

Here's a classic "risk" essay—only admissions officer 1 found anything redeeming in it. And yet it is a careful and accomplished parody of Dostoevsky's *Notes from the Underground*, whose narrator is one of the most intriguingly disagreeable characters in fiction. The chance he took was that the readers might not be up on their Russian lit and might mistake the character's voice for the applicant's own (as my panelists did, in fact). But he wrote what he wanted to write, and he clearly had a good time doing it. It was also not the first parody he had ever written. Does it show enough about the writer? It shows he reads carefully and writes well (the imitation is very good), has a sense of humor, and goes his own way, though he's perhaps a little too well-defended. (Somebody on an admissions committee stood up for this guy; he was admitted Early Action from the Just Folks group to a college that takes just twenty percent of its applicants.) But three out of four admissions officers missed it. Beware: Good parodies are written by people who like to read and have a good ear for imitation. I have seen other good ones—an interview report on an applicant, supposedly written by James Joyce, comes to mind. The *real* lesson to learn from this one is that, if you are going to write a parody, the subject should not be the application process, but some other part of your life.

(G) Tell us anything you think we should know.

I try to spend all my time valuably. This summer I worked at a trucking company as a secretary in the accounting department. I found this to be a fulfilling job dealing with people and exposing me to the business world, which is where I would like to work in the future.

In most of the professions that are offered today math is used in some way, and during my school years I have always enjoyed studying math and science. These two subjects have also been my strongest points. I like to work with math in many ways, as I did this summer, and I also enjoy taking extra courses to increase my personal knowledge in math. While I worked I also took a calculus course in summer school, even though I had never taken precalculus.

I have used my spare time at school to create many different fundraising ideas to help the senior class raise money. These activities are important to the class and I enjoy the feeling of leadership associated with working for the good of everyone. (In fact, I have often been able to use my skills in math to aid in this process.)

While I am not in school I enjoy sitting in my room and drawing pictures of persons or objects that happen to be nearby. During the winter things that I really enjoy are skating and taking flying lessons in a Cessna 152.

I have matured a great deal since I was a sophomore. I came from a public school and at first the adjustment was difficult. But because I hate sitting around and being inactive, I soon got involved in many facets of school life. I like to always be doing something constructive.

I believe that every person can be more valuable by using his or her time more constructively. So many problems arise from people who are wasting their lives and feel they have nothing to do, as is shown by welfare. Hopefully through college I will be able to dedicate myself to being a productive member of society and I look forward to this opportunity.

1. Mindless non-sequiturs, but mercifully short at least.

2. Boring rehash, tells me nothing I don't already know.

3. Unimaginative drudge of an essay. I wouldn't wish this person on my worst enemy as a roommate.

4. Pretty basic, earnest, simple essay, somewhat unsophisticated. Sounds like a nice kid.

(H) Any topic.

In 1979 we moved to New York. Only then did I realize why I had spent the first twelve years of my life not fitting in. I was born in Tumalo, Oregon, literally a one-street town west of the Cascade Mountains in Oregon's "Dry Country." The people of Tumalo lived there because they had always lived there. Many of them didn't have the imagination or means to move.

My dad, on the other hand, did have the imagination and the means. A rebellious painter, he had fled an eastern society up-bringing for the "real-people" in Oregon and set up a studio there—a loft with white walls, wooden floors and plenty of light—where he played the guitar and painted what the townspeople called "that queer modern art." Everybody else wore a cowboy hat, plowed fields, trained horses and baled hay during the week; on weekends, they rode bucking broncoes.

My parents liked it there, but I knew early on that we weren't really part of things in Tumalo. I didn't milk a cow until my best friend, who woke to that chore every day, showed me how. I never did learn how to gather eggs or cream butter or ride horses, because I was too embarrassed to try something for the first time that all the other kids knew how to do from birth. I began to wonder why we didn't have cows to milk and horses to ride instead of books to read and oil paints and canvas to play with.

Kids need to fit in, and I did what I could. I remember strutting desperately around the rodeo grounds in my cowboy boots and jeans, happy and dusty from the powdery earth, guzzling an Orange Crush. In my memory I can still feel the cool lip of the bottle against my teeth and the sweet liquid. "At least I look like a cowgirl," I thought. A voice crackled out of the loud speaker announcing the best barrel rider and the best calf; I went over to the arena and cheered with my friend as her father came charging out of the pen on a white Palomino, right on the tail of a small black goat. I wanted *my* father to rope a goat from horseback, knock it to the ground, tie its four legs together faster than anybody else, then tip his Stetson to the crowd, spit some tobacco juice and cowboy-walk out of the arena.

I wanted more from my mother, too. It took me a long time to forgive her for my lunches. Little did she know the ordeal I went through every day with my daily cargo of ethnic foods and brown bread and organic peanut-butter sandwiches and carrots and celery; she refused to buy Wonder Bread and Twinkies. Every day in the lunchroom at Tumalo Elementary, I threw it all away without even taking it out of the bag.

My dad just wasn't going to be a cowboy, and my mother wasn't a cowboy's wife. They were Wellesley and Princeton graduates who wanted a simple life. But I don't think they realized what being different did to me. As adults, they could handle it and appreciate it. But I was the one who didn't have a heifer to enter in the 4-H competition.

I understand now what my parents wanted—the peace, the country, the howls of the coyotes at night, the absence of cocktail parties, a place where they could wear jeans and old work boots all week and didn't have to be social and send Christmas cards to business associates. I can appreciate all that now, but I was still glad when we moved to 112th Street and Broadway in a town where my friends—like me—ate souvlaki, kasha, bagels and tofu, and where modern art has a whole museum.

1. The best kind of autobiographical approach—one topic, well-covered, with a nice sense of perspective and atmosphere, providing a good feel for who the writer is.

2. I like the frustrated cowgirl. Enough spunk to make an effort and enough understanding to know why it didn't work. Interesting background. She knows herself well enough to conduct a thorough college search. She'll land on her feet. As long as she's not still annoyed with her folks, she's easy.

3. Solid essay giving some sense of the person. Quite helpful in assessing the candidate as a person.

4. Elegant, mature, and insightful essay about growing up as an outsider. *Wonderful!*

(I) Any topic.

A SENSE OF HUMOR

I consider a sense of humor to be the most important quality anyone can possess. One does not have to be uproariously funny to see the irony in a situation. Though I am an unassuming person, I enjoy making an appropriate humorous comment at times, while still maintaining a serious attitude toward the subject.

Humor is important in numerous situations, often helping to put another person at ease. For example, in the case of an athletic captain, the ability to make a person laugh, whether he be coach or player, will most often result in a better team spirit and performance of that person. It is doubtful that a captain who is "all business" can do an adequate job of leadership involving so many different personalities on the playing field. I have found this to be true of my participation on the soccer team, for instance.

Humor also helps in appreciating the lighter side of a bad situation. Sometimes "gallows humor" can be detrimental, but it often can help cheer up a victim of a crime or one who has lost a close relative. Many people are able to laugh through their tears and thus bear their misfortunes.

Maybe the ability to laugh at oneself is most valuable of all. If one makes a mistake, the quickest way to get over the experience is by making a joke of it. I think I have learned this lesson best from my mother. When I was growing up, joking often emerged as a key element in our exchanges. I found myself learning how to tease and, more importantly, how to be teased and not take myself so seriously.

As I have matured and become involved in social and other activities, I sometimes found myself in situations that were uncomfortable and not always under my control.

Often I have supplied an application of humor at tense or uncomfortable moments. I discovered that this technique makes interaction so much easier.

Sometimes, during stressful times at school, my friends comment amazedly that I am still able to laugh. I can only respond that humor has caused me to be able to put things in perspective. I am confident it will continue to prove invaluable, in college and beyond.

1. Has managed to take humor and turn it into cream cheese on white. A vapid unintelligent job.

2. Humorless.

3. This discussion of humor convinces me this character has none. Too self-absorbed a piece to be helpful or interesting.

4. Not particularly thoughtful or insightful.

(J) Any topic.

There is nothing that can prepare you to meet a future stepmother. One night my dad told me he wanted to take me out to dinner with a "special friend" of his. When Dad pulled up in the car, I was surprised because dinner with Dad usually meant a walk around the corner to Al Buon Gusto for pizza or spaghetti, or sometimes to Hunan Park for egg rolls and lo mein. "Oh," I thought, standing at the curb and seeing a sweep of red hair occupying my usual seat in the Olds, "a *special* friend."

"Liz," he beamed, "THIS is EVELYN!" It was dark in the car and I couldn't see her distinctly. Just as well . . . I was embarrassed by his enthusiasm. I knew he had girlfriends, but I had never been asked to meet one before. Special Friend. "Special" buzzed through my head like a dentist's drill.

We went to a chi-chi restaurant—exposed bricks, hanging plants, sawdust on the floor. Waiting for a table, we got our first good look at each other. She was what the fashion magazines call "petite." She had tiny, delicate features, bright auburn hair in a TV starlet's coif, and ten perfectly manicured nails painted passionate pink. At six feet, I'm used to feeling taller than other women but this was ridiculous. Her painfully high heels brought her up only to my shoulder and the longer we stood waiting for a table the bigger and clumsier I felt.

I had nothing to say to her . . . to them. I slouched against the brick wall eating peanuts from the bar, avoiding small talk, and cringed when Dad abandoned us to check on our table. We tried to talk.

"Oh, look, Liz," she said. "There's sawdust on the floor; that's such a special touch. Your dad is amazing to find such a gem in this kind of neighborhood."

She oozed compliments about how "special" it was for a girl to be six feet tall. "I envy big girls like you who can just wear anything." Her compliments only made me feel more like a mountain. I wanted to sink into a hole and escape.

It felt like Dad had been gone ten years, but finally he returned and the waiter found us a table in the corner. I sat like a zombie while they tried desperately to include me in their conversation. Dad encouraged me to talk about a past summer at a tennis camp. I guess he thought that would be a subject Evelyn and I could discuss. "Evelyn is such a wonderful little tennis player," he said.

Talking to people, especially unfamiliar or difficult people, is usually stimulating, but it was a struggle with Evelyn. Maybe one reason was the way they turned their names into a rhyme—she called him "Kev," and he called her "Ev."

"Ev," I discovered over dessert, had a talent for talking, not just dressing, in clichés. Everything was "special." "This is a really special place," she would say. Or, "You're a very special person." Or, "This is such a special evening."

They got married a little over a year ago. My dad seems very happy, so since then I've been working on my tolerance. It isn't always easy. I'm their most frequent dinner guest and movie companion, but I still can't help cringing a little when I hear the word "special."

1. A sensitive handling of a difficult situation. Meeting mom's replacement can't be easy and her attitude bespeaks real maturity and poise.

2. This is painful. If the family troubles haven't upset the school work, OK. (Let's also check with the women's basketball coach. Is she really six feet tall?)

3. This essay wimped out at the end. The subject is a good one and got mostly strong treatment with good insight and humor. I like the effort, especially its human quality.

4. The discomfort of meeting father's "special" friend is effectively portrayed but gives little insight into Liz beyond that. Sounds a bit bitter, alone? Tough being a teenager.

(K) If you could travel through time and interview any historical figure, whom would you choose, what would you ask, and why?

Throughout history, mankind has been beset by myriad wars and other violence. That is why my choice for an interview would be Martin Luther King, the non-violent pacifist who is an important example to us all. Dr. King exhibited many elements of commitment which can be shown to be lacking today, as well as values to which everyone would readily assent. He did much in his quest for equality and peace, finally winning the Nobel Peace Prize in 1964.

I would like to question Dr. King about his methodology, particularly in respect to effective organization for altering the existing status quo. This is because Dr. King's endeavors occurred in the realm of politics as well as religion. Since having worked on the newspaper I am particularly interested in being active politically in the future, so I would hope to discern something of the relative effectiveness of his approach in contrast to other such approaches. I would like to discover whether given the preconceived knowledge that his activities would cause his own untimely passing away, he would operate in the same manner. My guess would be affirmative, as a result of the fortitude he exhibited in many areas, even being incarcerated in jail at one point.

He would also be asked whether he thought that all children today in America, regardless of race, color or creed, are able to mature in an atmosphere of growth in which to realize their full potential, as Dr. King dreamed of

twenty years ago. Another inquiry would concern the idea
of non-violence, or rather violence, and whether the latter
can function at any time as an approach for certain of those
who are the underprivileged and seeking a solution for their
grievances, for instance in the case of South Africa.
    Asking these questions would be of benefit to many
due to the paucity of such figures as Dr. King today who are
truly trying to ameliorate current problems in our troubled
world. Dr. King explored every avenue and left no stone
unturned in his efforts to terminate discrimination in this
country and it would be an honor and a privilege to meet
him and allow him to air his views.

1. No one can write more clearly than he thinks, I suppose.
Turgid and cliché-ridden, the statement seems crafted with an
elementary school history text in one hand and a thesaurus in the
other.

2. Not much vitality here but an honest effort. This is a
tough choice, and I admire that.

3. Awkward use of language. Classic intellectually disem-
bodied high school effort. Totally devoid of depth or insight.

4. Poorly written, excessively formal.

Number 2's puzzling reaction tells much. Here is a mindless
essay, almost inconceivably bad. The lead is meaningless: because there have been wars, therefore I am choosing King to
interview? And the rest is worse—big words to no purpose. What
is he saying? Yet an admissions officer at a highly competitive
school strung along with it just fine. Mr. Windbag would probably
be caught by a second reader, but you never know. You would
probably do better not trusting to such luck. Write a good one.

(L) Tell us anything you think we should know.

I do some of my best thinking in the bathroom. I don't
mean to embarrass anyone by talking about something so
private, but it's probably a good thing for you to know in
case we begin a four year relationship in which I'll have to
do a lot of thinking.
    The reason I'm going public with this announcement is

that this fall I began to see I wasn't the only one who felt inspired and peaceful in that small room where we are alone with our bodies and our thoughts. My dad, for instance, calls it the reading room. He thinks he's joking, but I noticed the bathroom is actually the *only* place he reads now. He says he's just too busy to take time for luxuries like novels. (He means in his life outside the bathroom.) My other connection was learning last year in art history class that Toulouse Lautrec, the French painter, once wanted to hang his pictures in the men's room of a restaurant so they would be fully appreciated. "It is the most contemplative moment in a man's day," he said.

I've always tried to be a good son and a good student, and so for a while I followed Dad's example and Lautrec's suggestion and passed time in the bathroom by reading or looking at pictures. But that changed one day when Mom, in a cleaning frenzy, had cleared out all the magazines and books and I wound up in there alone with the tiles and the towels. Pretty soon I got tired of reading the monograms on the face cloths and turned to the window, which looks out over a bit of lawn toward a few trees beside our house. Seated (I promise not to be crude), I wasn't thinking of anything except how bored I was. Then suddenly I was thinking of many things at once: a good opening paragraph for my history paper, a new way to look at a chemistry problem I'd been working on, even the perfect gift for my girlfriend's birthday, just to mention the more practical. I also had other thoughts rushing across my mind like clouds in a windy sky: the meaning of long-forgotten conversations, sudden connections between very different ideas. It came out of nowhere and it was exhilarating. I felt like a philosopher. Since then I haven't read a word in there; I just assume the pose of Rodin's Thinker and let it happen. I guess some of it may be just physiology (Dad says I have an "awesome metabolism"), but there's more to it than that, a fact I learned when I once tried bringing a pad in to make some notes; it only ruined the spell. Sometimes now I write down what I can remember afterward, but the thinking I do in the bathroom is pure and undistracted, and the way to do it is to do nothing.

I get the sense from news programs I've seen that

world leaders don't spend enough time in the bathroom, let alone do much thinking there. Like my dad, they're just too busy with realities to afford the luxury of pure reflection. As a result, I don't hear many exhilarating thoughts coming out of world leaders these days, nothing that shows much imagination or excitement. Just the same old deadlock on the same deadly issues. They're always flying around the world, sending guns or warnings to one another, disrupting their digestions and never taking the time between all those briefings to sit down and make peace with their own biology, never mind with other countries. Even when they're home, security reasons probably prevent them from having bathrooms with much of a view. I bet the White House even has a telephone in the bathroom. That would be the worst. Maybe that's why world leaders all look so constipated, even when they smile.

I think we'd all be better off if once a day we pumped all the heads of state full of apple cider—Dad says it's "nature's laxative"—and locked them for twenty minutes in small rooms with a good view of some trees, or a hill, or a pond, or a bird's nest, away from telephones and briefings and realities. Maybe they'd think of something.

1. In its own bizarre way this essay manages to be appealing. Reminiscent of Russell Baker, someone smart has started with an ordinary notion and played it out effectively. His wry sense of humor works well.

2. This is fun. He's funny. And I'd like to meet the father. All other things being equal, I'd want him in my class and in my dorm. Wise and funny, with an interesting perspective on things. He'll be conscientious without taking it all too seriously.

3. Good expansion of humorous subject into the verities of everyday life and world events. Some clever language here. A case of humor and self-revelation working to good end.

4. Sensitive, quite thoughtful. Some potentially crude parts in their graphic quality, but sincere and genuine. Does seem to be thinking. Good job.

In every good essay, the sentences and words are simple, the thinking vivid, the images detailed. The same can be said of the professional pieces in the following chapter. Ultimately, you will stay on course if you keep in mind the image of a young and otherwise energetic admissions officer stooping like a stuffed pelican over a lump of undigested applications. It is midnight. Wearily he opens the evening's thirty-eighth folder. "I do some of my best thinking," begins the essay, "in the bathroom." The admissions officer smiles a little. He is restored to life.

So is the applicant.

12 Anthology

It would probably surprise many professional reporters and editors to know that they write college essays for a living, or at least dabble now and then in the form. (They have a weird idea that it's "journalism.") Look through the opinion pages and special sections of newspapers and magazines and you'll see what I mean: column after column of short, personal, and pointed pieces that would help (if their grades and recommendations checked out) sneak them into old First Choice U.

The college essay flourishes in the hands of many writers. Only a few are represented here. I recommend that you seek out longer essays as well, not only by the writers below but also by George Orwell, Tom Wolfe, Joan Didion, Stephen Jay Gould, John McPhee, Woody Allen, G. K. Chesterton, and many, many others.

I've included two by E. B. White, because he really was the master of the college essay. I realize you may never write as well as E. B. White; not many of us do. But, as Yogi Berra said, "You can observe a lot just by watching." The way to get better, in writing as in baseball, is to keep your eye on the pros. Study their moves, pick up their tricks, imitate them if you like. As contradictory as it sounds, imitation is one of the quickest paths toward finding your own voice. Though he was talking about painting, the words of Pablo Picasso, the most original of artists, apply equally to writing: "You should constantly try to paint like someone else. But the thing is, you can't! You would like to. You try. But it turns out to be a botch. . . . And it's at the very moment you make a botch of it that you're yourself." In the selections below you'll hear a variety of distinctive voices. They were not written as college essays, but they could have been. That's because, although the pieces didn't "get them in" anywhere (except perhaps into our minds and hearts), they "work."

All the essays that follow could be used for the "Tell us anything you think we should know" or "Write on any topic you like" assignments. But the first three could also be responses to "Discuss a problem of national or international concern."

E. B. WHITE *Heavier than Air*

The first time I ever saw a large, heavy airplane drop swiftly out of the sky for a landing, I thought the maneuver had an element of madness in it. I haven't changed my opinion much in thirty years. During that time, to be sure, a great many planes have dropped down and landed successfully, and the feat is now generally considered to be practicable, even natural. Anyone who, like me, professes to find something implausible in it is himself thought to be mad. The other morning, after the Convair dived into the East River, an official of the Civil Aeronautics Board said that the plane was "on course and every circumstance was normal"—a true statement, aeronautically speaking. It was one of those statements, though, that illuminate the new normalcy, and it encouraged me to examine the affair more closely, to see how far the world has drifted toward accepting the miraculous as the commonplace. Put yourself, for a moment, at the Convair's controls and let us take a look at this day's normalcy. The speed of a Convair, approaching an airport, is about a hundred and forty miles an hour, or better than two miles a minute. I don't know the weight of the plane, but let us say that it is heavier than a grand piano. There are passengers aboard. The morning is dark, drizzly. The skies they are ashen and sober. You are in the overcast. Below, visibility is half a mile. (A few minutes ago it was a mile, but things have changed rather suddenly.) If your forward speed is two miles per minute and you can see half a mile after you get out of the overcast, that means you'll be able to see what you're in for in the next fifteen seconds. At the proper moment, you break out of the overcast and, if you have normal curiosity, you look around to see what's cooking. What you see, of course, is Queens—an awful shock at any time, and on this day of rain, smoke, and shifting winds a truly staggering shock. You are close to earth now, doing two miles a minute, every circumstance is normal, and you have a fifteen-second spread between what you *can* see and what you can't. What you hope to see, of course, is Runway 22 rising gently to kiss your wheels, but, as the passenger from Bath so aptly put it, "When I felt water splashing over my feet, I knew it wasn't an airport."

Airplane design has, it seems to me, been fairly static, and designers have docilely accepted the fixed-wing plane as the sensible and natural form. Improvements have been made in it, safety devices have been added, and strict rules govern its flight. But I'd like to see plane designers start playing with ideas less rigid than those that now absorb their fancy. The curse of flight is speed. Or, rather, the curse of flight is that no opportunity exists for dawdling. And so weather is still an enormous factor in air travel. Planes encountering fog are diverted to other airports and set their passengers down hundreds of miles from where they want to be. In very bad weather, planes are not permitted to leave the ground at all. There are still plenty of people who refuse to fly simply because they don't like to proceed at two miles a minute through thick conditions. Before flight becomes what it ought to be, a new sort of plane will have to be created—perhaps a cross between a helicopter and a fixed-wing machine. Its virtue will be that its power can be used either to propel it rapidly forward or to sustain it vertically. So armed, this airplane will be able to face bad weather with equanimity, and when a pall of melancholy hangs over Queens, this plane will be seen creeping slowly down through the overcast and making a painstaking inspection of Runway 22, instead of coming in like a grand piano.

JOHN UPDIKE   *Beer Can*

This seems to be an era of gratuitous inventions and negative improvements. Consider the beer can. It was beautiful—as beautiful as the clothespin, as inevitable as the wine bottle, as dignified and reassuring as the fire hydrant. A tranquil cylinder of delightfully resonant metal, it could be opened in an instant, requiring only the application of a handy gadget freely dispensed by every grocer. Who can forget the small, symmetrical thrill of those two triangular punctures, the dainty *pffff*, the little crest of suds that foamed eagerly in the exultation of release? Now we are given, instead, a top beetling with an ugly, shmoo-shaped "tab," which, after fiercely resisting the tugging, bleeding fingers of the thirsty man, threatens his lips with a dangerous and hideous hole. However, we have discovered a way to thwart Progress, usually so unthwartable. *Turn the beer can upside down and open the bottom.* The bottom is still the way the top used to be. True, this operation gives the beer an unsettling jolt, and the sight of a consistently inverted beer can might make people edgy, not to say queasy. But the latter difficulty could be eliminated if manufacturers would design cans that looked the same whichever end was up, like playing cards. What we need is Progress with an escape hatch.

E. B. WHITE   *The Age of Dust*

On a sunny morning last week, I went out and put up a swing for a little girl, age three, under an apple tree—the tree being much older than the girl, the sky being blue, the clouds white. I pushed the little girl for a few minutes, then returned to the house and settled down to an article on death dust, or radiological warfare, in the July *Bulletin of the Atomic Scientists*, Volume VI, No. 7.

The article ended on a note of disappointment. "The area that can be poisoned with the fission products available to us today is disappointingly small; it amounts to not more than two or three major cities per month." At first glance, the sentence sounded satirical, but a rereading convinced me that the scientist's disappointment was real enough—that it had the purity of detachment. The world of the child in the swing (the trip to the blue sky and back again) seemed, as I studied the ABC of death dust, more and more a dream world with no true relation to things as they are or to the real world of discouragement over the slow rate of the disappearance of cities.

Probably the scientist-author of the death-dust article, if he were revising his literary labors with a critical eye, would change the wording of that queer sentence. But the fact is, the sentence got written and published. The terror of the atom age is not the violence of the new power but the speed of man's adjustment to it—the speed of his acceptance. Already, bombproofing is on approximately the same level as mothproofing. Two or three major cities per month isn't much of an area, but it is a start. To the purity of science (which hopes to enlarge this area) there seems to be no corresponding purity of political thought, never the same detachment. We sorely need, from a delegate in the Security Council, a statement as detached in its way as the statement of the scientist on death dust. This delegate (and it makes no difference what nation he draws his pay from) must be a man who has not adjusted to the age of dust. He must be a person who still dwells in the mysterious dream world of swings, and little girls in swings. He must be more than a good chess player studying the future; he must be a memoirist remembering the past.

I couldn't seem to separate the little girl from radiological warfare—she seemed to belong with it, although inhabiting another sphere. The article kept getting back to her. "This is a novel type of warfare, in that it produces no destruction, except to life." The weapon, said the author, can be regarded as a horrid one, or, on the other hand, it "can be regarded as a remarkably humane one. In a sense, it gives each member of the target population [including each little girl] a choice of whether he will live or die." It turns out that the way to live—if that be your choice—is to leave

E. B. WHITE　*The Age of Dust (continued)*

the city as soon as the dust arrives, holding "a folded, damp-
ened handkerchief" over your nose and mouth. I went outdoors again to push the swing some more for the little girl,
who is always forgetting her handkerchief. At lunch I
watched her try to fold her napkin. It seemed to take
forever.

As I lay in bed that night, thinking of cities and target
populations, I saw the child again. This time she was with
the other little girls in the subway. When the train got to
242nd Street, which is as far as it goes into unreality, the
children got off. They started to walk slowly north. Each
child had a handkerchief, and every handkerchief was prop-
erly moistened and folded neatly—the way it said in the
story.

The next few essays are different responses to the request
"Please tell us something about yourself."

RUSSELL BAKER　*Summer Beyond Wish*

A long time ago I lived in a crossroads village of northern
Virginia and during its summer enjoyed innocence and
never knew boredom, although nothing of consequence
happened there.

Seven houses of varying lack of distinction constituted
the community. A dirt road meandered off toward the
mountain where a bootleg still supplied whiskey to the men
of the countryside, and another dirt road ran down to the
creek. My cousin Kenneth and I would sit on the bank and
fish with earthworms. One day we killed a copperhead
which was basking on a rock nearby. That was unusual.

The heat of the summer was mellow and produced
sweet scents which lay in the air so damp and rich you could
almost taste them. Mornings smelled of purple wisteria,
afternoons of the wild roses which tumbled over stone
fences, and evenings of honeysuckle.

Even by standards of that time it was a primitive place. There was no electricity. Roads were unpaved. In our house there was no plumbing. The routing of summer days was shaped by these deficiencies. Lacking electric lights, one went early to bed and rose while the dew was still in the grass. Kerosene lamps were cleaned and polished in an early-morning hubbub of women, and children were sent to the spring for fresh water.

This afforded a chance to see whether the crayfish population had multiplied. Later, a trip to the outhouse would afford a chance to daydream in the Sears, Roebuck catalogue, mostly about shotguns and bicycles.

With no electricity, radio was not available for pacifying the young. One or two people did have radios that operated on mail-order batteries about the size of a present-day car battery, but these were not for children, though occasionally you might be invited in to hear "Amos 'n' Andy."

All I remember about "Amos 'n' Andy" at that time is that it was strange hearing voices come out of furniture. Much later I was advised that listening to "Amos 'n' Andy" was racist and was grateful that I hadn't heard much.

In the summer no pleasures were to be had indoors. Everything of delight occurred in the world outside. In the flowers there were hummingbirds to be seen, tiny wings fluttering so fast that the birds seemed to have no wings at all.

In the heat of midafternoon the women would draw the blinds, spread blankets on the floor for coolness and nap, while in the fields the cattle herded together in the shade of spreading trees to escape the sun. Afternoons were absolutely still, yet filled with sounds.

Bees buzzed in the clover. Far away over the fields the chug of an ancient steam-powered threshing machine could be faintly heard. Birds rustled under the tin porch of the roof.

Rising dust along the road from the mountains signaled an approaching event. A car was coming. "Car's coming," someone would say. People emerged from houses. The approaching dust was studied. Guesses were hazarded about whom it might contain.

Then—a big moment in the day—the car would cruise past.

"Who was it?"

"I didn't get a good look."

"It looked like Packy Painter to me."

"Couldn't have been Packy. Wasn't his car."

The stillness resettled itself as gently as the dust, and you could wander past the henhouse and watch a hen settle herself to perform the mystery of laying an egg. For livelier adventure there was the field that contained the bull. There, one could test his courage by seeing how far he dared venture before running back through the fence.

The men drifted back with the falling sun, steaming with heat and fatigue, and washed in tin basins with water hauled in buckets from the spring. I knew a few of their secrets, such as who kept his whiskey hidden in a mason jar behind the lime barrel, and what they were really doing when they excused themselves from the kitchen and stepped out into the orchard and stayed out there laughing too hard.

I also knew what the women felt about it, though not what they thought. Even then I could see that matters between women and men could become very difficult and, sometimes, so difficult that they spoiled the air of summer.

At sunset people sat on the porches. As dusk deepened, the lightning bugs came out to be caught and bottled. As twilight edged into night, a bat swooped across the road. I was not afraid of bats then, although I feared ghosts, which made the approach of bedtime in a room where even the kerosene lamp would quickly be doused seem terrifying.

I was even more afraid of toads and specifically of the toad which lived under the porch steps and which, everyone assured me, would, if touched, give me warts. One night I was allowed to stay up until the stars were in full command of the sky. A woman of great age was dying in the village and it was considered fit to let the children stay abroad into the night. As four of us sat there we saw a shooting star and someone said, "Make a wish."

I did not know what that meant. I didn't know anything to wish for.

ELLEN GOODMAN *A Failure of Faith in Man-Made Things*

There are those who have faith in man-made things and those who do not.

I do not.

I do not have faith in elevators. I do not have faith in planes, subways, bridges or tunnels.

I do use them. Of which fact I am very proud.

I have, for example, a friend who chose his dentist because the dentist's office was on the first floor. I know a journalist who became a national expert on trains because he can't bear flying. I have another friend who sold his island house after living there only weeks because he had dizzy spells on the bridge. (The alternative route—a tunnel—was completely out of the question.)

I don't think these people are neurotic. Rather, it's a question of degree. How many of the rest of us travel on, over and through man-made things comforted only by our private *escape* plans?

That's the dividing point. People who have faith in man-made things do not have escape plans. I do.

I have an escape plan for the elevator. I will escape Certain Death if the elevator drops twenty floors suddenly—which I fully expect—because I will be jumping up and down. I read once that if you jump up and down while the elevator is crashing you have a 50 percent chance of being up while it's down and softening the impact.

Don't tell me if it's not true.

I have an escape plan for the final subway stall. If somewhere between stops the transit line dies and there are four hundred of us squeezed into one car so tightly that no one can move an arm to break a window, I will escape. I will be at my usual post, nose in the door, gasping the one thin stream of air as it comes through a crack.

On the whole, I am more philosophical about airplanes. I look quite relaxed: seated, belted (no, I never take off my seatbelt, not even between here and Paris) and read-

ELLEN GOODMAN   *A Failure of Faith (continued)*

ing a paper before takeoff. I repeat ten times, "Well, it's out of my hands now." But look closer. I am in the last row, because I remember from a Jimmy Stewart movie, *The Phoenix,* that you've got the best chance of surviving near the tail. I will *escape.* If I weren't so concerned about looking cool, I would ride on the plane's rear lavatory floor.

As for bridges, I remember the Galloping Gertie. Other bridges look sturdy enough, but there is only one railing between me and the water. When I drive over them, I roll up my window, because if my car plunges into the water—it is possible, it really is—there will be an air bubble in it. I will be able to breathe until I collect myself and then execute a perfect *escape* like the ones you see on television.

Don't tell me if it isn't true.

My greatest phobia is about tunnels—maybe because my escape plans stink. Every time I go through a tunnel, I expect the Ultimate Leak. And I haven't figured any way out against the rising water except (1) drive for it or (2) run for it.

I do try to control myself. After all, I have driven through two thousand tunnels without even using the windshield wipers. But I am prepared for the worst.

I don't know how tunnels are built, or bridges, or elevators, or airplanes. I don't know how or why they work. So why should I believe they're safe? How do I know they won't break with me on, in, or over or under them?

My escape plans are nothing more than an attempt at control. I know that I don't want to be dependent on the metal of a bridge, or the concrete of a tunnel. In truth, I don't really want to depend on man-made things at all. I hate being that far from Control Center. A severe failure of faith.

I suppose I would make one lousy astronaut.

H. L. MENCKEN   *Introduction to the Universe*

At the instant I first became aware of the cosmos we all infest I was sitting in my mother's lap and blinking at a great burst of lights, some of them red and others green, but most of them only the bright yellow of flaring gas. The time: the evening of Thursday, September 13, 1883, which was the day after my third birthday. The place: a ledge outside the second-story front windows of my father's cigar factory at 368 Baltimore Street, Baltimore, Maryland, U. S. A., fenced off from space and disaster by a sign bearing the majestic legend: AUG. MENCKEN AND BRO. The occasion: the third and last annual Summer Nights' Carnival of the Order of Orioles, a society that adjourned *sine die*, with a thumping deficit, the very next morning, and has since been forgotten by the whole human race.

At that larval stage of my life, of course, I knew nothing whatever about the Order of Orioles, just as I knew nothing whatever about the United States, though I had been born to their liberties, and was entitled to the protection of their army and navy. All I was aware of, emerging from the unfathomable abyss of nonentity, was the fact that the world I had just burst into seemed to be very brilliant, and that peeping at it over my father's sign was somewhat hard on my still gelatinous bones. So I made signals of distress to my mother and was duly hauled into her lap, where I first dozed and then snored away until the lights went out, and the family buggy wafted me home, still asleep.

DAVID OWEN   *Pfft*

In my mind I am seventeen, although in actual fact—in man-made years—I am older. When I go to pick up baby-sitters, I think of them as young contemporaries, the way eleventh-graders think of ninth-graders. They, in contrast, think of me as a crumbling historical specimen. "I wish my dad would ever wear a jacket like that," one of them said not long ago. She didn't mean (it turned out) that she thought I looked sharp; she meant that she wished her father would stop trying to dress so youthfully.

A couple of years ago in New York, I was walking down Seventieth Street wearing blue jeans, sneakers, and

DAVID OWEN   *Pfft (continued)*

an old sweatshirt. Two boys in their late teens were playing football on the sidewalk. The ball got away from them and rolled to my feet. I bent to pick it up and toss it back. One of the boys said, "I'll get that, sir."

I am so used to being thought of as a member of the Young Generation that the idea of becoming a member of the Old Generation is pretty hard to accept. This feeling seems to be widely shared. Lately I have noticed that people my age usually teach their children to address grown-ups by their first names. I am Dave or Davey to my daughter's friends, not Mr. Owen. This may be just a change of fashion, like the day in 1964 when my father and every other man in America stopped wearing a hat. But I think it's something else. Some of my friends don't even like to be called Mom or Dad. I can understand this. When my daughter calls me Dave, as she does occasionally, I am as thrilled as I was when I went to the front door recently and a salesman asked, "Are your parents home?"

My daughter turned two not long ago. I said to her, "Here's how old you are: One, two. Now here's how old Daddy is: One, two, three, four, five, six, seven, eight, nine, ten, eleven, twelve, thirteen, fourteen, fifteen, sixteen, seventeen [pause], eighteen, nineteen, twenty, twenty-one, twenty-two, twenty-three, twenty-four, twenty-five, twenty-six, twenty-seven, twenty-eight, twenty-nine, thirty, thirty-one." This made me feel depressed. To make myself feel better, I told her how old Grandpa is.

When my daughter was born, one of her great-grandfathers said, "I don't mind being a great-grandfather, but I can't stand being the father of a grandfather."

When I was twenty-one, I asked my father, who was fifty-one at the time, how old he felt. "Not very," he said. I asked, "How long ago does it seem since you were my age?" He thought for a moment, and then waved his hand and said, "Pfft."

The next two essays are "specialty" responses.

If you could interview anyone, living or dead, whom would you choose, what would you ask, and why?

ANDY ROONEY *Questions for the President*

There are some things about any President of the United States we never get to know. Partly it's because it's none of our business, but partly it's because no one ever asks the President those questions. If I could have a fifteen-minute interview with Ronald Reagan, here are some of the things I'd ask him:

—First, Mr. President, what are the three things you'd least like to talk about?

—Is being President as good as you thought it would be?

—What do you hate most about it?

—Do you think you could ever go back to making movies?

—If one of the big studios offered you ten million dollars and a piece of the action to make a film in 1985, would you be tempted to accept the offer instead of running for reelection? Twenty million dollars?

—Have you sneaked out of the White House at all without any protection?

—Who's the biggest jerk you've met in government? Democrat or Republican?

—How's the lung, still hurt? Not even when you laugh about it? You remember that joke?

—How much money do you carry on you? Ever have a chance to spend any of it?

—Could we just have a look at what you carry in your pockets and in your wallet?

—You like the water on the warm or on the cool side when you take a shower?

—I'm tired of this jelly bean thing. How do you feel about it?

—You dress beautifully except for your shirt collars. You have a fifteen-and-a-half neck, but you wear a size seventeen collar. How come?

—How many suits do you own? Do you know? How many pairs of shoes, or have you lost track of this sort of thing since you've been President? Does a President ever wear out a piece of clothing?

—You often read without glasses. Do you wear contacts?

—Would you just briefly explain the difference between Afghanistan and Pakistan?

—How do you handle your mail? Don't you miss going to the front door for it? Is it embarrassing not to have time to read letters from old friends? Do you ever sit down and write a letter to an old friend who hasn't written you, just for the hell of it?

—How's your spelling? Your arithmetic?

—I mean this as a general question. I'm not suggesting you're dumb, but how do you account for the fact that the smartest person in the United States doesn't get elected President? What do *you* have that the smartest person doesn't have that makes us all want you for the job?

—Tell me what you think of when I mention the following names:

> John Dean
> Henry Kissinger
> Billy Martin
> Jesus Christ
> Jean Harlow. She would have been exactly your age.
> Jacqueline Kennedy Onassis. Ever met her?
> Picasso
> Linda Ronstadt
> Mike Wallace

Thank you, Mr. President!

Describe an achievement, experience, or interest that is important to you.

FRAN LEBOWITZ   *Why I Love Sleep*

I love sleep because it is both pleasant and safe to use. Pleasant because one is in the best possible company and safe because sleep is the consummate protection against the unseemliness that is the invariable consequence of being awake. What you don't know won't hurt you. Sleep is death without the responsibility.

The danger, of course, is that sleep appears to be rather addictive. Many find that they cannot do without it and will go to great lengths to ensure its possession. Such people have been known to neglect home, hearth, and even publishers' deadlines in the crazed pursuit of their objective. I must confess that I, too, am a sleeper and until quite recently was riddled with guilt because of it. But then I considered the subject more carefully and what I learned not only relieved my guilt but also made me proud to be among the fatigued.

I would like to share my findings so that others might feel free to lay down their once uplifted heads. I have therefore prepared a brief course of instruction in order to instill pride in those who sleep.

THE FRAN LEBOWITZ SLEEP STUDIES PROGRAM

Sleep is a genetic rather than an acquired trait. If your parents were sleepers, chances are that you will be too. This is not cause for despair but rather for pride in a heritage that you share not only with your family but also with a fine group of well-known historical figures. The following list is indicative of the diversity to be found among sleepers:

SOME WELL-KNOWN HISTORICAL FIGURES WHO WERE SLEEPERS

Dwight D. Eisenhower

While many remember Ike (as he was affectionately called by an adoring nation) for his golf, there is little doubt but that he was a sleeper from childhood, a trait he unquestionably carried with him to the White House. In fact, so strongly committed was he to sleep that one could barely distinguish Ike's sleeping from Ike's waking.

William Shakespeare

Known as the Bard among his colleagues in the word game, Shakespeare was undoubtedly one of literature's most inspired and prolific sleepers. Proof of this exists in the form of a bed found in the house he occupied in Stratford-Upon-Avon. Further references to sleeping have been discovered in his work, and although there is some question as to whether he actually did all his own sleeping (scholarly debate currently centers around the possibility that some of it was done by Sir Francis Bacon), we are nevertheless safe in assuming that William Shakespeare was indeed a sleeper of note.

e. e. cummings

The evidence that e. e. cummings was a sleeper is admittedly sparse. Therefore, it is generally accepted that he was perhaps more of a napper.

It is only to be expected that if so many well-known historical figures were sleepers, their accomplishments should be of equal import. Following is a partial list of such achievements:

SOME CONTRIBUTIONS TO WORLD CULTURE
MADE BY SLEEPERS

Architecture
Language
Science
The wheel
Fire

I rest my case.